Preface

Welcome to the incredible world of Artificial Intelligence Class 6 (AI), a rapidly evolving field reshaping our lives, work, and interactions with the world around us. This book has been specially designed for class six students to serve as an engaging and accessible introduction to the fascinating domain of AI. As you embark on this journey, you will begin to uncover the remarkable potential of AI and its profound impact on various aspects of modern life. This book aims to make AI understandable and approachable for young learners. In an era where technology is a driving force behind many of the changes we see, it is essential to start building a solid foundation of knowledge at an early age. This book has been crafted with the belief that by introducing students to AI concepts and engagingly, we can spark curiosity and foster an enthusiasm for learning that will serve them well in future.

What you will find in this book:

Clear and Simplified Explanations:

AI concepts are broken down into easy-to-understand explanations, ensuring you can grasp the fundamentals without feeling overwhelmed.

Real-World Applications:

Discover how AI is used in everyday life, from voice assistants to recommendation systems, across various fields like healthcare, education, entertainment, etc.

Ethical Considerations:

Explore the ethical questions AI raises, such as privacy, job displacement, and decision-making biases, and understand the importance of responsible AI use.

Interactive and Hands-On Learning:

Engage with activities and projects that reinforce your understanding of AI concepts and allow you to apply what you've learned in a fun and creative way.

Our Vision:

We aim to spark a genuine interest in AI, encouraging you to explore and learn more about this fascinating field. This book provides a solid foundation, setting the stage for more profound studies and future opportunities in AI and related areas. We hope to cultivate your curiosity and inspire you to discover AI's endless possibilities.

Table of Contents

Chapter 1: Introduction to AI

Learning Objectives

Understand what Artificial Intelligence (AI) is.
Difference between Human and Machine Intelligence.
AI applications in different areas.
Branches, Advantages and Disadvantages of AI.

1.1 Understanding Artificial Intelligence (AI)

Imagine if you had a robot friend who could play your favourite games with you, help you finish your homework, and even chat with you just like a real person. This might sound like something out of a science fiction movie, but thanks to something called Artificial Intelligence, or AI, it's actually possible!

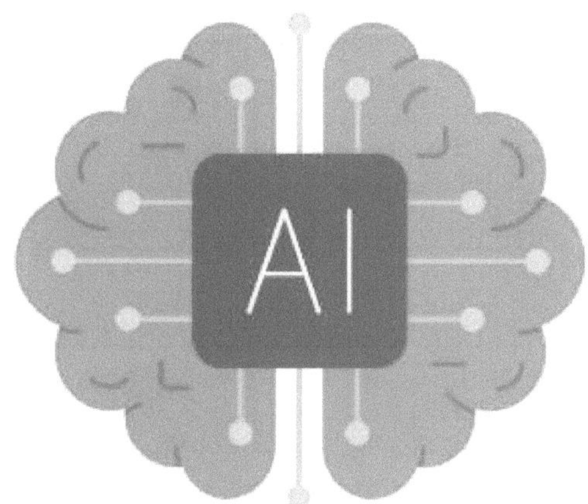

Artificial Intelligence (AI) is a special kind of technology that allows machines—like computers, robots, and even smartphones—to think and learn in ways similar to humans. Just like how you learn new things every day—whether it's solving a tricky Math problem or learning how to ride a bicycle—AI helps machines learn from their experiences. This means that over time, these machines can get better at tasks, recognise patterns, and even make decisions on their own.

How Artificial Intelligence (AI) works:
AI operates by learning from data. Large data sets teach machines how to make decisions or recognise patterns. For instance, AI might analyse thousands of pictures of cats to know what a cat looks like. Once it learns from the data, it can identify a cat in a new picture.

Key features of Artificial Intelligence (AI):
Learning: AI systems can improve their performance over time through learning from data.
Reasoning: AI can make decisions based on available information, similar to human reasoning.
Problem solving: AI can solve complex problems by analysing patterns and drawing conclusions.
Perception: AI systems can interpret and understand data from their surroundings, like recognizing objects in an image or understanding speech.

For example, have you ever asked your smartphone's voice assistant, like Siri or Google Assistant, to play your favourite song? When you do that, AI will work behind the scenes. It helps the voice assistant understand your request and find the song you want to hear. This is just one of the many ways AI makes our lives easier and more fun!

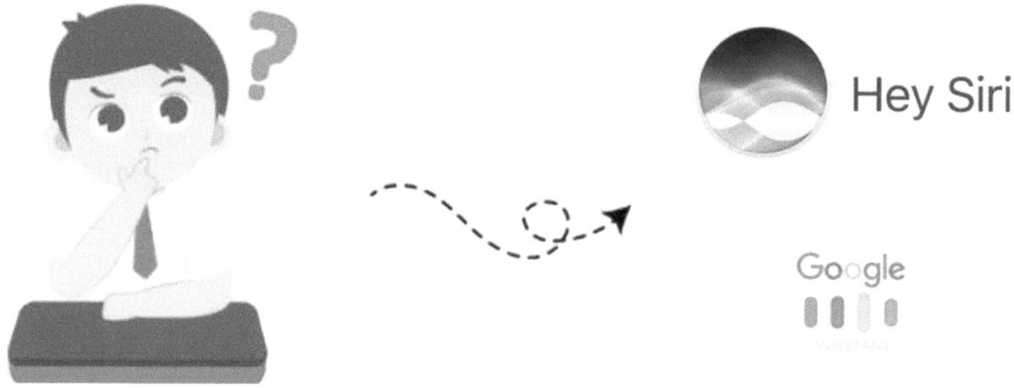

AI is becoming more and more common in the world around us. From the apps on your phone to the smart devices in your home, AI is a big part of modern life, helping to make things more convenient and enjoyable. As you learn more about AI, you'll discover how powerful and fascinating this technology is!

Definition - Artificial Intelligence (AI) is when computers or machines can think and learn like humans, helping them perform tasks like recognising images, understanding language, and making decisions.

1.2 Need for Artificial Intelligence (AI)

Artificial Intelligence is increasingly necessary because it can handle tasks that are difficult, time-consuming, or even impossible for humans to perform manually. Here are some critical reasons for the growing need for AI:

Automation:
AI can automate repetitive tasks, allowing humans to focus on more complex and creative work. For example, factories use AI-powered robots to assemble products, reducing the need for manual labour.

Handling Big Data:
AI can quickly process vast amounts of data. This is particularly useful in fields like healthcare, where AI can analyse medical records to detect patterns that might go unnoticed by human doctors.

Improving decision-making:
AI helps in making better decisions by analysing data and predicting outcomes. For example, AI helps businesses decide what products to sell by analysing customer preferences and market trends.

Increased efficiency and speed:
AI can complete tasks more quickly and with fewer errors than humans. For instance, AI processes thousands of transactions per second in banking to detect fraudulent activity.

Makes life easier:
AI makes everyday tasks more manageable by helping us find information quickly, giving reminders, or suggesting what we might like, just like an intelligent assistant.

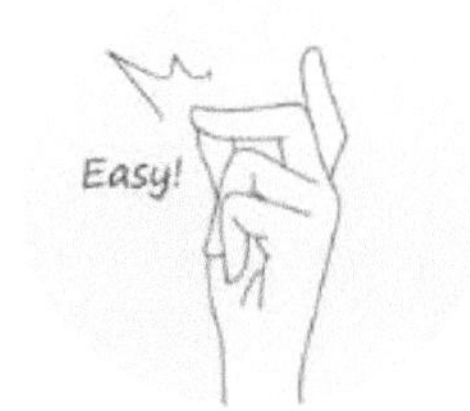

Assists in difficult jobs:
AI can perform tasks that are too difficult or dangerous for humans, like exploring deep oceans or outer space, making it invaluable in risky situations.

Solves big problems:
AI helps solve complicated problems by quickly analysing large amounts of data, which is especially useful in fields like healthcare for diagnosing diseases.

Learns from experience:
AI improves by learning from its experiences, much like how we improve at something with practice. This ability to learn makes AI increasingly effective at what it does.

Example:
Imagine visiting a website and needing help finding something or tracking your order. Instead of waiting for a person to reply, a friendly AI-powered chatbot will help you instantly. You can ask the chatbot any question, like "When will my package arrive?" and it will check the information and give you an answer right away. It works 24/7, so the chatbot is always ready to help, even if you ask at night.

Amazingly, this chatbot can talk to many people simultaneously, answering questions for hundreds of users without getting tired. It can also understand different languages, so people from all over the world can get help quickly. By taking care of simple tasks, AI chatbots allow human workers to focus on more complicated issues, ensuring everything runs smoothly and efficiently.

1.3 Human and Machine Intelligence

Human Intelligence

Human Intelligence is our natural ability to think, learn, and solve problems. It helps us understand the world, make decisions, and interact with others. Humans can also feel emotions, be creative, and generate new ideas.
For example, you're using your Intelligence to decide what to wear based on the weather. You also use your intelligence to learn new things, like how to ride a bike or solve a Math problem.

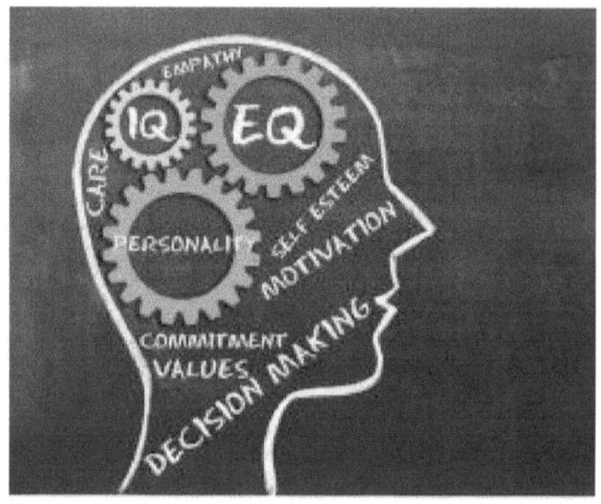

Machine Intelligence
On the other hand, Machine Intelligence is the ability of machines, like computers and robots, to perform tasks that usually require Human Intelligence. However, machines do this differently. They don't have emotions or creativity like humans do. Instead, they follow instructions given to them by humans.
These instructions are called Algorithms, which are like step-by-step guides. Machines use data to learn and get better at tasks over time, but they do this by processing information quickly and following the rules set by their programming.

Difference between Human and Machine Intelligence

Feature	Human Intelligence	Machine Intelligence
Emotions and feelings	Humans can feel emotions like happiness, sadness, and love.	Machines do not have emotions or feelings.
Creativity	Humans are creative and can develop new ideas, draw, write, and invent.	Machines can only do what they are programmed to do; they cannot create new ideas independently.
Learning	Humans learn from experiences, mistakes, and others.	Machines learn by processing data and following rules (algorithms).
Decision-Making	Humans make decisions based on knowledge, emotions, and experiences.	Machines make decisions based on data and instructions; they don't have feelings.
Flexibility	Humans can adapt to new situations and think of solutions to unexpected problems.	Machines are good at the specific tasks they are programmed for but may struggle with unexpected situations unless they are specifically programmed for them.

1.4 Applications of Artificial Intelligence (AI)

Artificial Intelligence (AI) is not just a concept; it's something we use daily, often without even realising it. Here are some simple examples of how AI is used in the real world:

Healthcare:
AI helps doctors diagnose diseases by analysing medical images, predicting patient outcomes, and suggesting treatment options. AI can even assist in surgeries, guiding surgeons with precise, data-driven insights, etc.

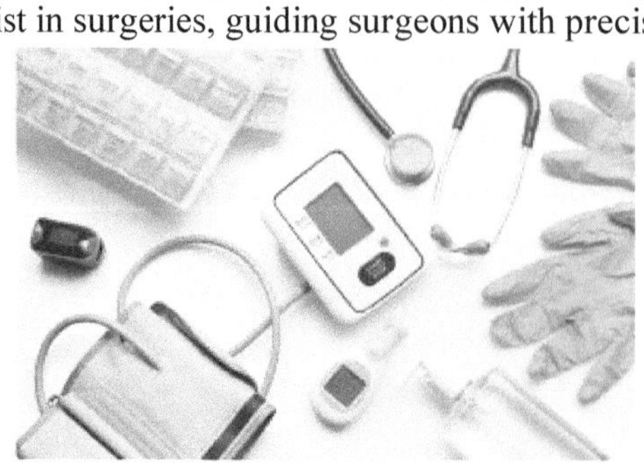

Education:
AI tools help teachers create personalised learning experiences for students. AI-powered platforms can track student progress and suggest lessons tailored to the student's needs.

Transportation:
AI is used in self-driving cars to detect obstacles, follow traffic rules, and navigate roads. AI also helps manage traffic systems in smart cities, reducing congestion and improving road safety.

Customer service:
AI-powered chatbots provide real-time customer support on websites. These chatbots can answer common questions, solve problems, and help customers make purchases.

Entertainment:
Streaming platforms like Netflix and YouTube, use AI algorithms to recommend content based on users' viewing habits. AI also creates music, writes stories, and even paints.

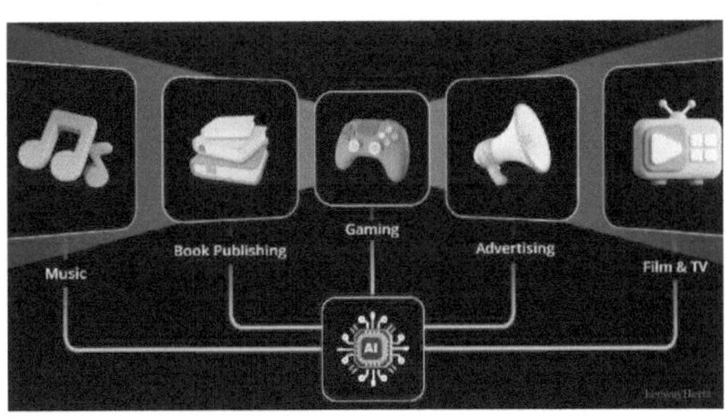

Fun fact:
AI helped create the famous "Portrait of Edmond de Belamy," a machine-generated painting that sold for over $400,000.

1.5 Branches of Artificial Intelligence (AI)

Artificial Intelligence is a vast field, and it is divided into several branches, each focusing on a different aspect of making machines more intelligent. Let's explore the main branches of AI:

Machine Learning (ML):
Machine Learning is an AI that allows computers to learn from data and improve over time without being programmed for every specific task. Computers study data, learn from it, and make decisions based on it.
Example:
If you use a streaming service like Netflix, the app recommends movies or shows based on what you've watched previously. This is Machine Learning in action!

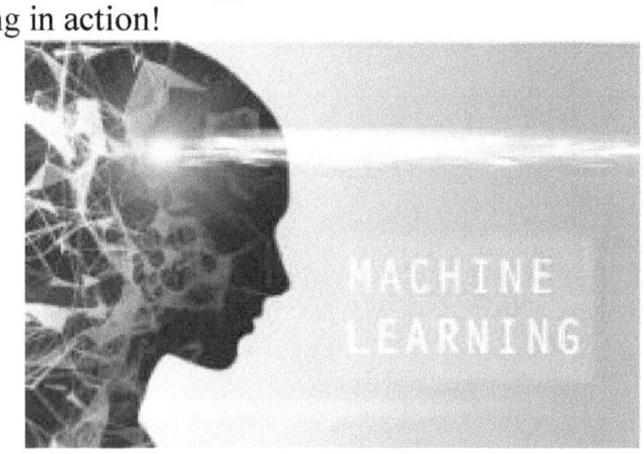

Natural Language Processing (NLP):
NLP helps machines understand and communicate in human language. This allows computers to read, listen, and even respond to our speech or text, allowing us to talk to machines like others.
Example:
When you ask Alexa or Google Assistant to play your favourite song, they understand your request through NLP and respond accordingly.

Robotics:
AI is used in robots to help them perform physical tasks. Robots can be programmed to assemble products, explore dangerous areas, or even assist in surgeries.
Example:
Robots are used in factories to assemble cars or electronics, doing tasks that are too repetitive or risky for humans.

Computer Vision:
Computer Vision allows AI to "see" by interpreting and understanding images or videos. AI recognises objects, faces, or even hand-written text using this branch.
Example:
Face recognition in smartphones uses Computer Vision to unlock the phone by recognising the user's face.

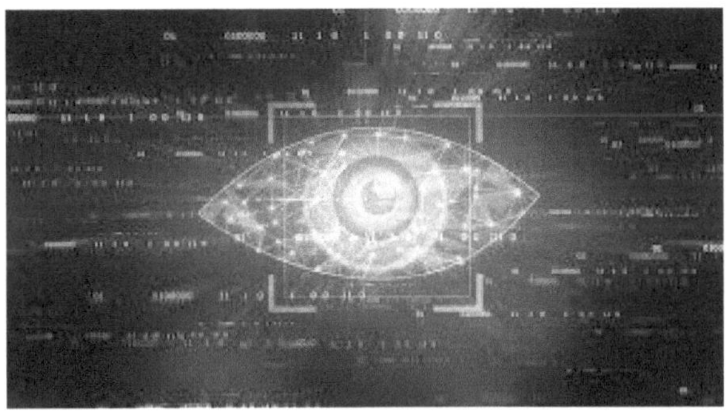

Deep Learning:
Deep Learning is a type of Machine Learning that uses neural networks designed to mimic the human brain. It helps AI understand complex data and perform speech and image recognition tasks.
Example:
AI that can identify pictures of animals or even diagnose diseases from X-rays uses Deep Learning to learn from thousands of examples.

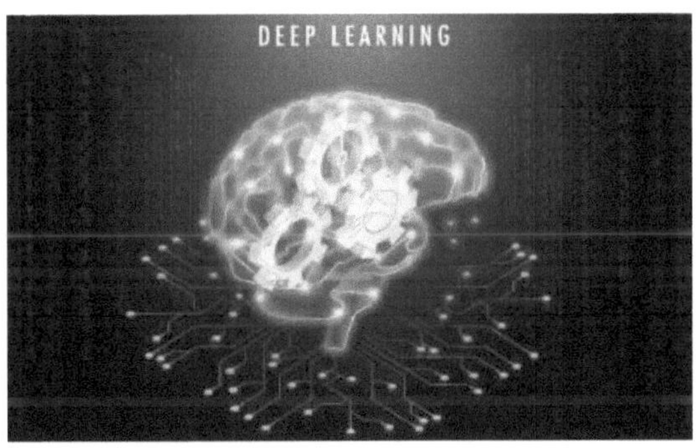

1.6 Advantages and Disadvantages of Artificial Intelligence (AI)

Advantages of Artificial Intelligence (AI):
AI brings many benefits to our world. Here are some of the key advantages:

Efficiency and speed:
AI can process large amounts of data much faster than humans. It can handle repetitive tasks quickly and without getting tired, which increases productivity and reduces errors.
Example:
AI systems in banks can process thousands of transactions per second, checking for fraud and managing accounts faster than a human could.

24/7 Availability:
Unlike humans, AI systems don't need to sleep or take breaks. This means AI can work around the clock, offering services anytime people need them.
Example:
Customer service chatbots provide help at any hour of the day, ensuring customers always get the support they need, even late at night.

Accuracy and precision:
AI reduces the chance of human errors in tasks. It can perform calculations and analyse data more accurately than humans, especially with large datasets.
Example:
AI can assist doctors in healthcare by analysing medical images and detecting diseases with high accuracy, sometimes better than the human eye.

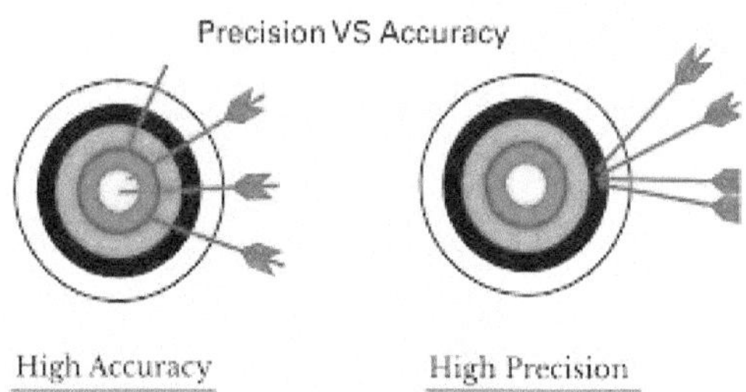

Learning and improvement:
Through Machine Learning, AI systems improve over time as they learn from new data, making them more useful the longer they are used.
Example:
Voice assistants like Siri or Alexa improve as they learn how you speak and your preferences, making their responses more personalised.

Handling complex tasks:
AI can analyse and solve complex problems by processing vast amounts of data. This is useful in areas like scientific research, where AI helps solve challenging problems humans alone can't handle.
Example:
AI is used in climate science to analyse weather patterns and predict future climate changes.

Disadvantages of AI:
While AI offers many advantages, there are also some drawbacks to using it. Here are some key disadvantages:

Lack of emotions:

AI cannot feel emotions or understand human feelings. This limits its use in areas where empathy or emotional understanding is needed, such as counselling or teaching.

Example:

A robot or AI system can't comfort someone feeling sad like a human could.

High cost:

Creating and maintaining AI systems can be expensive. It requires a lot of resources to develop AI software, collect and manage data, and ensure that the systems are working correctly.

Example:

Building a self-driving car requires advanced technology, sensors, and robust AI software, making it costly.

Dependence on Data:

AI relies heavily on data. The AI system can make wrong decisions if the data used to train the AI is biased, incomplete, or inaccurate. AI needs high-quality data to perform well.

Example:

If an AI system is trained on biased data, it might make unfair decisions, like favouring one group of people in the hiring process.

Job displacement:

As AI systems take over specific tasks, there is a concern that they could replace human jobs, especially in manufacturing, customer service, and data processing.

Example:

AI-powered robots in factories might replace workers who used to assemble products manually.

Ethical and Privacy concerns:
AI systems often require large amounts of data, including personal information. This raises privacy concerns about how that data is collected and used. There are also ethical concerns about AI decision-making in law enforcement or medicine.
Example:
Facial recognition systems used in public places can raise privacy issues if people are being watched without consent.

1.7 Summary

AI allows machines to think and learn like humans, improving over time.
Humans are emotional and creative, while machines follow programmed instructions.
AI makes our lives easier by letting us control devices with our voice, making games more fun, suggesting things to buy, helping cars drive by themselves, and supporting doctors in finding out what's wrong with patients.
AI improves speed, accuracy, availability, and problem-solving.
AI lacks emotions, can be costly, may cause job loss, and raises privacy concerns.

1.8 Glossary

Artificial Intelligence (AI): Technology that allows machines to think and learn like humans.
Voice Assistant: A digital helper, like Siri or Alexa, responds to spoken commands.
Algorithm: A set of step-by-step instructions a machine follows to complete a task.
Smart Devices: Gadgets like smartphones that use AI to perform tasks automatically.
Data: Information that AI systems use to learn and make decisions.
Pattern Recognition: AI's ability to identify and understand repeating patterns in data.
Ethical Concerns: Moral issues related to AI.
Job Displacement: Job loss due to AI taking over tasks.
Privacy Concerns: Issues about how AI uses personal data.

1.9 Exercise

Exercise 1 – Choose the correct answer from the given options.

1. What is Artificial Intelligence (AI)?
   a) A type of Human Intelligence
   b) A special kind of technology that allows Machines to think and learn like humans
   c) A game for robots
   d) A computer virus

2. Which of the following is an example of AI?
   a) Reading a book
   b) Playing soccer
   c) Using Siri to set an alarm
   d) Drawing a picture

3. How do Machines learn in AI?
   a) By going to school
   b) By following instructions called algorithms
   c) By watching TV
   d) By sleeping

4. Which is NOT true about Human Intelligence?
   a) Humans Intelligence can feel emotions
   b) Humans Intelligence can make decisions based on experiences
   c) Humans Intelligence can learn from mistakes
   d) Humans Intelligence can only do what they are programmed to do

5. What do self-driving cars use to understand the road?
   a) A map
   b) AI with cameras and sensors
   c) A compass
   d) The driver's manual

Exercise 2 – Check if the sentence is true or false.

1. AI can only be used in smartphones. …………..
2. Machines with AI can learn from Data and improve over time. …………..
3. Humans cannot adapt to new situations, but machines can. …………..
4. AI is used in video games to make the game more challenging. …………..
5. Human Intelligence includes creativity and emotions, while Machine Intelligence does not. …………..

Exercise 3 – Fill the blank space with the correct word.

1. Artificial Intelligence (AI) helps machines ……………. from their experiences and improve over time.
2. AI is used ………….. like Siri and Google Assistant, to understand and respond to our questions.
3. In video games, AI helps the computer learn how you play and then tries to ………….. you.
4. Unlike Machines, Humans can feel ………….. such as happiness, sadness, and love.
5. AI helps ………….. suggest products you might like based on what you have looked at or bought.

Exercise 4 – Answer the following questions in your own words.

1. What is Artificial Intelligence?
2. Give an example of how AI is used in everyday life.
3. What's the difference between Human and Machine Intelligence?
4. How does AI help in healthcare?
5. What are the advantages and disadvantages of Artificial Intelligence?

Exercise 5 – Solve the puzzle.

Find and circle the words listed below. Words can go in any direction—up, down, left, right, or diagonal.

ARTIFICIAL
MACHINE
LEARNING
VOICE
ALGORITHM
HUMAN

A	R	T	I	F	I	C	I	A	L	V
L	E	A	R	N	I	N	G	G	T	O
W	N	F	S	P	X	U	K	G	A	I
F	S	U	T	L	H	U	M	A	N	C
U	W	X	Q	Z	N	O	X	C	H	E
M	A	C	H	I	N	E	U	B	Y	N
A	L	G	O	R	I	T	H	M	L	D

1.10 Project Work

Link:https://www.youtube.com/playlist?list=PLzlh_31VWEFr7zLPrhw7NE1yJSoueINU5

QR Code:

Create your own AI storybook.

This project aims to introduce students to Artificial Intelligence (AI) basics through a creative and hands-on activity. By crafting a storybook that illustrates AI concepts, students will understand how AI can be applied in everyday situations, fostering both their creativity and critical thinking skills.

1.11 Group Discussion

Link: https://www.youtube.com/playlist?list=PLzlh_31VWEFpMfn6e1d5Foc-z9z5mEPpR

QR Code:

Exploring the impact of AI on our lives

This group discussion's objective is to help students explore how AI affects our lives, considering its benefits and challenges. It encourages them to share ideas, listen to others, and work together, all while deepening their understanding of AI and improving their communication skills.

1.12 Case Study

Link:
https://www.youtube.com/playlist?list=PLzlh_31VWEFou05BLESc_ypeORzkKbTcU

QR Code:

The AI Dilemma at Green Valley School

Background: Green Valley School in India wants to introduce Artificial Intelligence (AI) to help with learning and school management. They are considering using AI to grade exams, monitor classrooms, and assist students with homework. However, teachers, parents, and students have some concerns, which are given below.

The Problems:

Privacy: Parents worry that AI cameras watching students in classrooms could invade their privacy.
Fair Grading: Teachers are unsure if AI can correctly grade creative answers like essays or art projects.
Job Concerns: Some staff fear AI might replace their roles in the school.
Data Safety: The school is worried about how to keep student information safe from hackers or misuse.

1.13 Fun Activity

Activity: AI explorer

Objective:

This activity aims to help students recognise and understand how Artificial Intelligence (AI) is used daily. Through a simple exploration activity, students will learn to identify AI in everyday devices and applications, making AI more relatable and accessible.

Steps:

1. Introduction:

Explain to students that AI is a unique technology that helps machines think and learn like humans. Emphasise that AI is found in many things they use daily, such as smartphones, games, and websites.

2. AI Hunt:

Ask students to explore their home or classroom and find three examples of AI in use. These could include a voice assistant (e.g., Siri or Alexa), an online shopping website that recommends products, or a video game that changes difficulty levels based on how the player plays.

Students should write down what the AI does and how it helps make life easier or more fun.

Have students draw a picture of one of the AI examples they found. Then, they will share their drawing with the class and explain what the AI does and its usefulness.

3. Class discussion:

After all students have shared their examples, discuss how AI makes life easier and more enjoyable in various ways.

Discuss any new AI applications students might have learned about from their peers.

Learning outcomes:

Students will learn to identify AI in everyday objects and tools.

Students will gain a basic understanding of how AI functions in real-life applications.

Students will develop communication skills by sharing their findings with the class.

This activity is designed to be simple, engaging, and educational, helping students connect with the concept of AI in a fun and meaningful way.

And the best part? AI keeps getting better the more it learns! It's like having a tool that's always improving.
That's so cool! With AI, we can solve big problems and create amazing things.
Exactly! AI is opening up a world of possibilities, making life easier, more efficient, and a lot more exciting.
Let's start our own AI project! Imagine what we could create!
This is going to be so exciting! With AI, the future is bright and full of possibilities!
Absolutely! The sky's the limit with AI—we can achieve incredible things together!

Chapter-1

TEST PAPER
Introduction to AI

Time Duration: 30 Minutes
Maximum Marks: 20

General Instructions:

1. This paper consists of twelve questions and is divided into two sections: A and B.
2. All questions are compulsory.
3. Section A comprises MCQs, Fill in the blanks, True or False, and One word of one mark each.
4. Section B comprises answer the following questions with three marks each.

SECTION-A

I - Choose the correct answer from the given options. **(1 X 2 = 2 marks)**

1. What helps AI systems recognise patterns and make decisions?
   a) Books b) Data
   c) Toys d) Paintings
2. Which of the following tasks can AI NOT do?
   a) Write its own emotions b) Help diagnose diseases
   c) Recognize faces in photos d) Suggest products to buy online

II - Fill the blank space with the correct word. **(1 X 2 = 2 marks)**

1. AI systems follow a set of instructions called ____________ to perform tasks.
2. Unlike Humans, Machines do not have ____________, which means they cannot feel happiness or sadness.

III - Check if the sentence is true or false. **(1 X 2 = 2 marks)**

1. AI can help improve the safety of driving through self-driving cars.
2. Machines with AI can make decisions based on feelings and emotions.

IV - Write the answer in one word. **(1 X 2 = 2 marks)**

1. What is the term for the information AI uses to learn and improve?
2. What are the step-by-step instructions that AI follows to complete tasks?

SECTION-B

V - Answer the following questions in your own words. **(3 X 4 = 12 marks)**

1. How does AI help in online shopping?
2. Why can't Machines experience emotions like Humans?
3. What role does AI play in social media?
4. What are the branches of AI?

Answer

Exercise 1- 1. b) **2.** c) **3.** b) **4.** d) **5.** b)
Exercise 2- 1. False **2.** True **3.** False **4.** True **5.** True
Exercise 3- 1. learn **2.** voice assistants **3.** challenge **4.** emotions **5.** online stores

Online Resources

Online Exam Paper Link:
Link: https://forms.gle/TLdLryz1Lz42HYsq5
QR Code:

Chapter 1 Videos Link:
Link: https://www.youtube.com/playlist?list=PLzlh_31VWEFo0YjhqJwoN8tF9YcbsPI8X
QR Code:

More Sample Test Paper

Chapter 1 Test Paper – 1 Link:
Link: https://forms.gle/Uaq2YBpNDiyV8Tct9
QR Code:

Chapter 1 Test Paper – 2 Link:
Link: https://forms.gle/t9c8HWz32nCembkd8
QR Code:

Chapter 1 Test Paper – 3 Link:
Link: https://forms.gle/5bBoPgkDvvMwLbPX6
QR Code:

Chapter 1 Test Paper – 4 Link:
Link: https://forms.gle/vpDQKrDsGeVhFB2eA
QR Code:

Chapter 2: Understanding Intelligence

Learning Objectives

Understand the Concept of Intelligence
Types of Intelligence
Features of Human Intelligence
Apply Ways to Enhance Intelligence

2.1 What is Intelligence?

Intelligence is like a superpower that everyone has! It helps us learn new things, solve problems, and understand the world around us. We can use our Intelligence to determine how to do things better and make good choices. Think of Intelligence as how our brain works to help us think, learn, and be creative.

We use muscles to lift things or run fast, and we use our Intelligence to think and solve problems.

For example, you use your Intelligence to figure out the solution when you solve a puzzle. When you learn something new at school, like a math problem or a science fact, your Intelligence helps you understand and remember it.

Intelligence is the ability to learn, think, solve problems, and understand the world around us. It helps us adapt to new situations and make decisions.

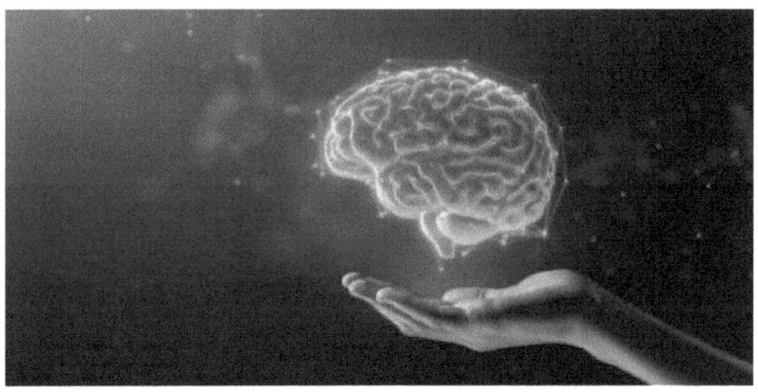

How Intelligence works:

Learning: Intelligence helps you learn new things, whether it's solving a math problem or learning how to play a musical instrument.

Understanding: It allows you to understand why things happen the way they do, like why plants need sunlight to grow.

Problem-solving: Intelligence helps you find solutions to challenges you face, like figuring out how to complete a tricky homework assignment.

2.2 Kinds of Intelligence

Did you know that everyone has a special kind of Intelligence? Here are some types of Intelligence that show how people can be innovative in different ways:

1. Logical Intelligence:

This is the ability to think logically and solve mathematical problems. People with this type of Intelligence are good at reasoning, puzzles, and understanding patterns.

Example:

You might have strong Logical Intelligence if you enjoy solving math problems or science experiments.

2. Linguistic Intelligence:
This intelligence is about using language—writing, reading, and speaking. People with solid linguistic Intelligence can easily express their thoughts and communicate with others.
Example:
You likely have high Linguistic Intelligence if you love reading books or writing stories.

3. Musical Intelligence:
This type of Intelligence allows people to understand and create music. Those with Musical Intelligence can quickly pick up rhythms, melodies, and tunes.
Example:
You probably have strong Musical Intelligence if you're good at playing an instrument or singing.

4. Spatial Intelligence:
People with this Intelligence are good at visualising and imagining things in their minds. They can think about spaces, shapes, and how things fit together.
Example:
You have solid Spatial Intelligence if you enjoy drawing or designing buildings with blocks.

5. Bodily-Kinaesthetic Intelligence:
This Intelligence involves controlling your body movements and using them to express yourself or solve problems. Athletes, dancers, and people who work with their hands often have strong bodily Intelligence.
Example:
A dancer expressing emotions through movement or a carpenter crafting furniture are examples of Bodily-Kinaesthetic Intelligence.

6. Interpersonal Intelligence:
This is understanding other people's emotions and working well in teams. People with this Intelligence are good at making friends and understanding what others need or feel.
Example:
If you're the person your friends come to for advice, you probably have high Interpersonal Intelligence.

7. Intrapersonal Intelligence:
This is about understanding yourself—your feelings, thoughts, and strengths. People with this Intelligence are good at reflecting on their emotions and setting personal goals.
Example:
If you are good at knowing what makes you happy or what you're good at, you have robust Intrapersonal Intelligence.

8. Naturalistic Intelligence:
People with this intelligence are deeply connected to nature and understand how the environment works. They enjoy learning about plants, animals, and the earth.
Example:
You might have naturalistic solid Intelligence if you love spending time in nature, learning about animals, or gardening.

2.3 Features of Human Intelligence

Human Intelligence is exceptional because it allows us to do things that machines or animals can't easily do. Here are some essential features of Human Intelligence:

Learning and Adaptability:
Humans can learn from experiences and adapt to new situations. For example, if you make a mistake while playing a game, you learn from it and do better next time.

Problem-solving:
Humans can think creatively and devise different ways to solve problems. Whether figuring out how to fix a broken toy or developing a new idea for a school project, intelligence helps us find solutions.

Memory:
Memory is an integral part of Intelligence. It helps us remember facts, skills, and experiences. For example, remembering how to tie your shoelaces is something you learned in the past and can apply anytime.

Creativity:
Human Intelligence includes creativity and the ability to generate new ideas or approaches. Artists, writers, and inventors use their creativity to create something new.

Emotions and Empathy:
Humans can understand and feel emotions like happiness, sadness, and empathy. This helps us connect with other people, share feelings, and build relationships.

Communication:
Human Intelligence allows us to communicate effectively with others, whether it's through spoken words, written text, or body language. This is key to working together and understanding each other.

How can we get more thoughtful?
Here are some fun and easy ways to make our brains even smarter:

Learn something new: Try to learn new things every day. You can read a book, watch an educational video, or try a new hobby.

Practice makes perfect: Just like practising a sport makes you better at it, practising math, reading, or music makes you smarter.

Ask lots of questions: Be curious! If you don't know something, ask about it. The more questions you ask, the more you'll learn.

Take care of your brain: Eating healthy food, getting enough sleep, and playing outside can help your brain stay strong and ready to learn.

2.4 Can Machines be Intelligent?

Yes, machines can be intelligent, but their intelligence works differently from Human Intelligence. Machines use Artificial Intelligence (AI) to learn from data, solve problems, and perform tasks. However, machines do not have emotions, creativity, or self-awareness like humans do.

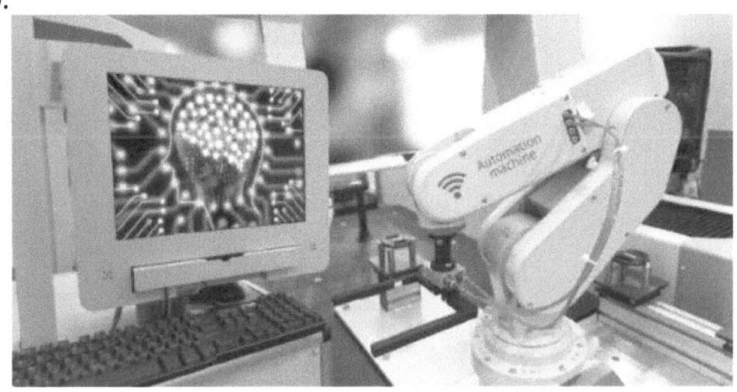

How Machine Intelligence works:

Machines use algorithms, which are sets of instructions, to learn and make decisions. For example, a computer program might learn to recognise different animals by analysing thousands of pictures of animals and understanding their differences.

Advantages of Machine Intelligence:

Speed: Machines can process information much faster than humans.

Accuracy: AI can follow instructions without making mistakes, making it useful for calculations or sorting large amounts of data.

Learning from Data: Machines can improve their performance by learning from new data.

Limitations of Machine Intelligence:

No emotions: Machines do not feel emotions like humans do. They can't understand happiness, sadness, or love.

No creativity: Machines cannot generate new ideas. They can only follow the rules programmed into them.

Dependence on Data: Machines can only learn from their given data. Without data, machines can't improve.

Example:

An AI-powered robot can help clean your house or answer simple questions but doesn't understand emotions or devise new cleaning methods. It simply follows the instructions it is given.

2.5 Why is Intelligence important?

Intelligence is vital for humans and machines because it helps us in many areas of life. Here's why intelligence is so valuable:

Problem-solving:

Intelligence helps us solve both simple and complex problems. Intelligence plays a significant role in finding the best way to build a tower out of blocks or make a city more eco-friendly.

Learning and growth:
Intelligence allows us to keep learning and growing. From learning to ride a bike to understanding new technology, intelligence helps us improve our skills and adapt to new challenges.

Creativity and Innovation:
With Intelligence, humans can create new inventions, write books, make music, and devise solutions that have never existed. It allows us to think outside the box and bring new ideas.

Understanding others:
Intelligence also helps us understand other people's emotions and feelings. This allows us to build strong relationships, work in teams, and care for others.

Efficiency and Productivity:
Machine Intelligence, like AI, helps humans by doing tasks faster and more accurately. AI can assist in factories, healthcare, education, and entertainment by speeding up processes and improving outcomes.

Making life easier:
Human and Machine Intelligence make life easier by helping us manage our time, solve problems, and accomplish goals. AI-powered devices like smartphones and smart homes help us stay organised and complete tasks quickly.

Example:
AI assistants like Siri or Alexa can help you set reminders, answer questions, or even play your favourite song, making your day more convenient.

2.6 Summary

Intelligence is our ability to think, learn, solve problems, and adapt to new situations.
There are different types of intelligence, like logical, verbal, musical, interpersonal, kinaesthetic, and naturalistic.
Intelligence is key to making good decisions and understanding the world.

2.7 Glossary

Adaptability: The ability to adjust to new situations or changes in the environment.
Creativity: The ability to generate new ideas, think outside the box, and create something original.
Empathy: The ability to understand and share the feelings of others.
Learning: The process of acquiring new knowledge, skills, or behaviours through study, experience, or teaching.
Problem-solving: The ability to find solutions to difficult or complex issues.

2.8 Exercise

Exercise 1 – Choose the correct answer from the given options.

1. What is Intelligence?
a) The ability to run fast
b) The ability to learn and solve problems
c) The ability to jump high
d) The ability to sleep

2. Which type of intelligence is related to math and solving puzzles?
a) Verbal Intelligence
b) Kinesthetic Intelligence
c) Logical Intelligence
d) Musical Intelligence

3. What is one thing that Machines cannot do like Humans?
a) Solve problems
b) Learn from data
c) Understand emotions
d) Process information quickly

4. Which type of Intelligence involves understanding and interacting with others?
a) Musical Intelligence
b) Interpersonal Intelligence
c) Naturalistic Intelligence
d) Logical Intelligence

5. Why is Intelligence important?
a) It helps us make better decisions
b) It makes us taller
c) It allows us to fly
d) It changes our eye colour

Exercise 2 – Check if the sentence is true or false.

1. Intelligence is only about being good at school subjects. ....
2. Machines can create art and music but do not have emotions. ....
3. Interpersonal Intelligence is about understanding nature. ....
4. Human Intelligence helps us adapt to new situations. ....
5. Machines can think creatively, just like humans. ....

Exercise 3 – Fill the blank space with the correct word.

1. People with .... Intelligence is good at solving puzzles and math problems.
2. .... Intelligence involves understanding and interacting well with others.
3. Machines can process information much .... than humans.
4. Intelligence helps us make good .... in life.

5. ……………… Intelligence is related to rhythm, melody, and sound.

Exercise 4 – Match each word or phrase in Column A with Column B.

Column A	Column B
1. Logical Intelligence	a) Creativity with music
2. Verbal Intelligence	b) Solving math problems
3. Kinaesthetic Intelligence	c) Writing and storytelling
4. Musical Intelligence	d) Sports and physical activities
5. Interpersonal Intelligence	e) Understanding others' feelings

Exercise 5 – Answer the following questions in your own words.

1. What is Intelligence, and how does it help us?
2. Name two types of Intelligence and describe them.
3. How do machines learn and solve problems?
4. Why can't machines understand emotions like humans?
5. How can you improve your Intelligence?

Exercise 6- List two examples for each given word.

1. Types of Human Intelligence: …………….. , …………….
2. Ways to improve Intelligence: …………….. , …………….
3. Examples of Machine Intelligence: …………….. , …………….
4. Skills developed by Kinesthetic Intelligence: …………….. , …………….
5. Things Humans can do but Machines can't: …………….. , …………….

Exercise 7- Look at the following pictures and identify the type of Intelligence each picture represents.

………………………… ………………………… …………………………

………………………… ………………………… …………………………

2.9 Project Work

Link: https://www.youtube.com/playlist?list=PLzlh_31VWEFrsoE-vXlg7M8hL3dAFcMkW

QR Code:

Invent your AI-powered gadget
To encourage creativity and innovation by having students design an imaginary AI-powered gadget that could help people in their daily lives.

2.10 Group Discussion

Link:https://www.youtube.com/playlist?list=PLzlh_31VWEFpTu1zTstM6-_q0o2qTsJoB

QR Code:

The power of Intelligence and AI
This group discussion aims to help students think about human intelligence, how people can be wise, and how machines can also be intelligent. Students will understand how humans and machines use intelligence uniquely by sharing their thoughts and ideas.

2.11 Case Study

Link:https://www.youtube.com/playlist?list=PLzlh_31VWEFo82SmngoC_iRP8fbT8I4dm

QR Code:

Intelligence in Humans and Machines
Scenario: Sana, a 12-year-old girl, is curious about what intelligence means for Humans and Machines. She notices her friends show different types of intelligence, like math or drawing, and wonders if her computer is "smart" like hers. Sana explores how humans and machines think, solve problems, and learn.
Key Issues:

- How do people show different intelligences (like logical or musical)?
- What makes Human Intelligence unique? Can Machines be "smart" like Humans?
- How do people and computers solve problems differently?
- Can both Humans and Machines learn? How do they learn?
- Can Machines be creative like Humans, or are they just following rules?

2.12 Fun Activity

Activity: AI Matching Game
Objective:
To help students understand different types of Artificial Intelligence (AI) by playing a matching game that connects AI applications to their functions in everyday life.
Materials Needed:

- Printed cards (or paper) with different AI applications and their descriptions.
- Scissors (to cut out the cards).
- A flat surface to play the game.

Steps:

- **Prepare the cards:**
  Create two sets of cards. One set contains different AI applications (like "Voice Assistant," "Self-Driving Car," "Online Shopping Recommender," etc.), and the other set includes descriptions of what these AI applications do (like "Helps you find products you might like" or "Plays music when you ask it to").
- **Match the AI to its function:**
  Shuffle the cards and lay them out face up. The student's task is to match each AI application to its correct description. For example, the card "Voice Assistant" should match the card "Plays music when you ask it to.
- **Group discussion:**
  After the game, gather the students and discuss why they matched specific AI applications with their functions. Talk about how these AI tools help in everyday life and where they might encounter them.
- **Optional extension:**

For added fun, students can create their own AI application and write a description for it. Then, they can trade cards with a classmate and try to match each other's AI ideas with the correct functions.

Example Cards:

AI application card: "Self-Driving Car".
Function card: "Drives you to your destination without needing a driver".
AI application card: "Voice Assistant".
Function card: "Helps you by setting reminders and answering questions".

SCENE - THE STUDENTS ARE SITTING & DISCUSSING WHAT THEY LEARNED ABOUT INTELLIGENCE IN THEIR RECENT CLASS.

Human intelligence is unique because it's so flexible. We can think logically, be creative, and understand feelings—all at once.
Can machines ever be as smart as us?
Machines can be smart in certain ways, like processing data or learning patterns. But they don't have the creativity or emotional understanding that we do.
So intelligence is important because it helps us grow and solve problems?
Exactly! It's our superpower, letting us innovate and make the world better.
I'm excited to learn more about how intelligence works.
I'm excited to learn more about how intelligence works. It's going to be an amazing journey!

Chapter-2
TEST PAPER
Understanding Intelligence

Time Duration: 30 Minutes
Maximum Marks: 20

General Instructions:

1. This paper consists of twelve questions and is divided into two sections: A and B.
2. All questions are compulsory.
3. Section A comprises MCQs, Fill in the blanks, True or False, and One word of one mark each.
4. Section B comprises answer the following questions with three marks each.

SECTION-A

I - Choose the correct answer from the given options. **(1 X 2 = 2 marks)**

1. Which of the following is NOT a type of Intelligence?
   a) Logical Intelligence
   b) Verbal Intelligence
   c) Physical Intelligence
   d) Musical Intelligence
2. What helps us make good decisions and solve problems?
   a) Speed
   b) Intelligence
   c) Strength
   d) Emotions

II - Fill the blank space with the correct word. **(1 X 2 = 2 marks)**

1. Musical Intelligence is about being good with __________, __________, and sound.
2. Machines can be programmed to solve specific __________.

III - Check if the sentence is true or false. **(1 X 2 = 2 marks)**

1. Human intelligence is only helpful in solving math problems.
2. Machines can understand human emotions just like people do.

IV - Write the answer in one word. **(1 X 2 = 2 marks)**

1. What type of Intelligence is involved in playing a musical instrument?
2. What feature of Human Intelligence helps us understand our emotions and those of others?

SECTION-B

V - Answer the following questions in your own words. **(3 X 4 = 12 marks)**

1. What is Intelligence, and how does it help us daily?
2. Describe the difference between Human Intelligence and Machine Intelligence.
3. Why is Verbal Intelligence critical in communication?
4. Give a few examples of how Logical Intelligence can be used in school.

Answer

Exercise 1- 1. b) 2. c) 3. c) 4. b) 5. a)
Exercise 2- 1. False 2. True 3. False 4. True 5. False
Exercise 3- 1. logical 2. interpersonal 3. faster 4. decisions 5. musical
Exercise 4- 1. b) 2. c) 3. d) 4. a) 5. e)

Online Resources

Online Exam Paper Link:
Link: https://forms.gle/FeEfgN1TuwaYE79s7
QR Code:

Chapter 2 Videos Link:
Link: https://www.youtube.com/playlist?list=PLzlh_31VWEFr_wPR2USYLq35na3Sf20Tk
QR Code:

More Sample Test Paper

Chapter 2 Test Paper – 1 Link:
Link: https://forms.gle/zuowsCakztnB92d47
QR Code:

Chapter 2 Test Paper – 2 Link:
Link: https://forms.gle/mCisXKM13MR1UJZq9
QR Code:

Chapter 2 Test Paper – 3 Link:
Link: https://forms.gle/XqpbfYftfnQp74Cy9
QR Code:

Chapter 2 Test Paper – 4 Link:

Link: https://forms.gle/cg1v71aCUijon57n8

QR Code:

Chapter 3: AI in Daily Life

Learning Objectives

Real-life Examples of AI
Virtual Assistant
AI in Entertainment
AI in Everyday Life

3.1 Understanding Real-Life Examples of Artificial Intelligence (AI)

Real-life examples of AI can be seen in various technologies we use daily. It is integrated into many tools and devices we use daily, making tasks more efficient and personalised. For example, virtual assistants like Siri or Alexa can understand and respond to voice commands, helping with tasks such as setting reminders or playing music. Self-driving cars use AI to navigate roads safely without human intervention. AI also powers smart home devices, like automated thermostats, which learn your preferences and adjust the temperature accordingly. These examples show how AI improves convenience, safety, and personalisation in our everyday lives.

Virtual assistants: Programs like Siri, Alexa, and Google Assistant can understand and respond to voice commands, helping with tasks like setting reminders, playing music, and controlling smart devices.
Self-driving cars: AI enables cars to navigate roads, avoid obstacles, and make driving decisions without human intervention, making transportation safer and more efficient.
Smart home devices: AI powers devices like automated thermostats and smart lights, learning your preferences and adjusting settings to make your home more comfortable.
Entertainment: AI recommends movies, music, and games based on your interests, helping you discover new content you'll enjoy.
These examples show how AI seamlessly integrates into our daily lives, making things more convenient, safe, and personalised. Now, let's understand these in detail.

3.2 Virtual Assistant

A virtual assistant is an intelligent computer program that helps you with tasks by understanding what you say or type. It uses Artificial Intelligence (AI) to listen to your commands, figure out what you want, and do it for you. You can find virtual assistants at home on your phone, computer, or even smart speakers. They make everyday tasks easier, like setting reminders, playing music, or controlling lights in your house.

Siri

Siri is Apple's virtual assistant, available on iPhones, iPads, Macs, and other Apple devices. To use Siri, you can say, "Hey, Siri," followed by your command. For example, if you want to know the weather, you can ask, "What's the weather today?" Siri will check the weather and provide you with the current conditions. Siri also learns from your usage patterns, like which apps you use most or who you frequently contact, to give you better suggestions and help.

Examples of tasks Siri can do:

Set reminders and alarms.
Send messages or make phone calls.
Provide directions or look up locations.
Control smart home devices like lights or thermostats.
Play music or podcasts.

Alexa

Alexa is Amazon's virtual assistant on devices like the Amazon Echo and other smart speakers. To use Alexa, you start by saying, "Alexa," followed by your request. For example, you can say, "Alexa, play my favourite playlist," and Alexa will play the music that matches your taste. Alexa can also control various smart devices in your home, like turning on lights, adjusting the thermostat, or locking doors. Over time, Alexa learns from your commands and becomes better at helping you with tasks.

Examples of tasks Alexa can do:

Play music or read audiobooks.
Control smart home devices.
Answer questions by searching the internet.
Provide news updates and weather forecasts.
Set timers and alarms.

Virtual assistants like Siri and Alexa are examples of how AI is used to make our lives more convenient and personalised.

3.3 AI in entertainment

AI is used in entertainment to make games, movies, and music more fun and exciting. It helps create realistic characters in video games, recommends films and songs you might like, and even helps artists create new music. AI can learn what you enjoy and suggest more things that match your tastes.

Movie recommendations

AI tracks what you've watched and enjoyed when you watch movies or TV shows on platforms like Netflix, Disney+, or Amazon Prime. It uses this information to recommend other movies or shows you like. For example, AI will suggest similar films if you enjoy superhero movies. This makes finding something fun to watch easier without spending a lot of time searching.

How AI helps:

Analyze your viewing history.
Suggests movies or shows that match your interests.
Keep your recommendations updated as your tastes change.

Video game characters
In video games, AI controls the behaviour of non-player characters (NPCs). These characters can interact with you in the game, making the experience more realistic and challenging. For example, AI might control other drivers in a racing game, making the race more exciting by adapting their driving styles to challenge you.

Examples of AI in games:
AI opponents in racing or shooting games.
Characters that react to your decisions in role-playing games.
Adaptive difficulty levels that match your skill level.

Music Suggestions
Music streaming apps like Spotify use AI to recommend songs and playlists based on your listening habits. When you listen to a song, the AI learns what music you enjoy and suggests similar songs. This way, you can discover new music that matches your taste without searching for it.

How AI helps:
Curates personalised playlists based on your listening history.
Recommends new artists and songs that you might like.
Updates suggestions as your music.

Social media
AI is also used in social media platforms like Instagram, Facebook, Twitter, etc. It helps show posts, ads, and content that match your interests. AI looks at what you view, like, comment on, and share and then suggests more of the same type of content.

Examples of AI in social media:
Recommends posts and videos that match your interests.
Filters out unwanted or inappropriate content.
Suggests friends or accounts you might want to follow.

AI in entertainment helps create personalised experiences, making finding content you'll love easier.

3.4 AI in everyday life

AI is not just limited to entertainment and virtual assistants; it also plays a vital role in everyday life, from typing messages to managing your smartphone's battery. Here are some examples:

Voice typing

Voice typing is a feature on smartphones and computers that uses AI to convert your speech into text. Instead of typing out a message or document, you can speak, and the AI will transcribe your words into text on the screen. This feature is handy for people with difficulty typing or needing to write something quickly.

Examples of Voice typing:

Dictating messages or emails.
Writing notes or documents by speaking.
Voice commands to search the web or control apps.

Battery management

Some smartphones use AI to manage battery life more efficiently. The AI learns how you use your phone throughout the day and adjusts power settings to make the battery last longer. For example, if you use your phone heavily in the evening, the AI might conserve power during the day to ensure you have enough battery life later.

How AI helps:

Analyses your phone usage patterns.
Adjusts brightness, background processes, and other settings.
Extends battery life by optimising power consumption.

Smart home devices

AI is used in various smart home devices, like thermostats, lights, security systems, etc. These devices learn your habits and preferences and automatically adjust settings to make your home more comfortable and secure. For example, a smart thermostat might know that you like it warmer in the morning and cooler at night and will adjust the temperature accordingly.

Examples of AI in smart homes:

Smart thermostats that learn your temperature preferences.
Automated lighting systems that adjust based on the time of day.
Security systems that recognise familiar faces and alert you to strangers.

Smartphones

AI enhances smartphone cameras by automatically adjusting settings like focus, lighting, and filters to improve your photos. For example, when photographing a sunset, the AI might enhance the colours to make the sky look more vibrant and beautiful.

How AI helps:

Improves photo quality by adjusting camera settings.
Recognises faces and objects to focus better.
Suggests filters and effects to enhance your photos.

Online shopping

When you shop online, AI helps you find products you might like by analysing your browsing and purchase history. It suggests items similar to what you've bought or searched for, making your shopping experience more personalised.

Examples of AI in online shopping:

Recommends products based on your past purchases.
Suggests items that other customers with similar tastes have bought.
Personalizes your shopping experience with targeted ads and offers.

AI is everywhere, from the devices we use to the services we enjoy. It helps us make tasks easier, improve convenience, and provide personalised experiences. By understanding how AI works in daily life, you can better appreciate the technology that powers our world and even think about how you might use AI to solve problems in the future.

3.5 Summary

AI allows machines to perform tasks requiring Human Intelligence, like learning and decision-making.
AI is present in virtual assistants, self-driving cars, and smart home devices, enhancing convenience and safety.
Siri and Alexa use AI to help with tasks through voice commands.
AI suggests movies and music and improves video game experiences based on user preferences.
AI helps with voice typing, battery management, smart home automation, and personalised online shopping.

3.6 Glossary

Virtual assistant: An intelligent program (like Siri or Alexa) that helps with tasks using voice commands.
Entertainment AI: AI used in games and movies to make them more fun and personalised.
Social media AI: AI that shows you posts and ads based on what you like on platforms like Instagram.
Smart home devices: AI-powered gadgets that learn your preferences and automate things like lighting and temperature in your home.
Online shopping: Buying products online with AI suggesting items based on preferences.
Personalization: AI tailoring services to individual preferences.

3.7 Exercise

Exercise 1 – Choose the correct answer from the given options.

1. What is an example of AI in everyday life?
 a) Virtual assistants like Siri and Alexa
 b) Manual typewriters
 c) Analog clocks
 d) Traditional radios

2. How do self-driving cars use AI?
 a) To play music
 b) To navigate roads safely without human intervention
 c) To charge their batteries
 d) To display advertisements

3. Which of the following is a smart home device that uses AI?
 a) Washing machine
 b) Automated thermostat
 c) Manual vacuum cleaner
 d) Non-digital alarm clock

4. AI helps in making tasks more _______.
 a) Difficult
 b) Efficient and personalised
 c) Time-consuming
 d) Expensive

5. AI improves _______ in our everyday lives.
 a) Convenience, safety, and personalisation
 b) Confusion and complexity
 c) Energy consumption
 d) Data loss

Exercise 2 – Check if the sentence is true or false.

1. AI is only used in computers. ....
2. Virtual assistants like Siri and Alexa can respond to voice commands. ....
3. Self-driving cars need a human driver to function. ....

4. AI in smart home devices can adjust the temperature automatically. ....
5. AI does not help in making tasks more efficient. ....

Exercise 3 – Fill the blank space with the correct word.
1. AI improves ...., safety and personalisation in our everyday lives.
2. Virtual assistants like Siri use .... to understand and respond to voice commands.
3. Self-driving cars use AI to navigate .... without human intervention.
4. .... is Apple's virtual assistant.
5. Alexa is a virtual assistant developed by ....

Exercise 4- Solve the jumbled word by arranging the letters.
1. RISI (Hint: Apple's virtual assistant)
2. XEALA (Hint: Amazon's virtual assistant)
3. RTHAMSOTET (Hint: A device that controls temperature)
4. NAGOITVAI (Hint: Helps find the fastest route)
5. ONLASERP (Hint: Recommendation of movies and shows)

Exercise 5- Write the answer in one word.
1. What is the name of Apple's virtual assistant?
2. What kind of cars use AI to drive themselves?
3. What technology helps in recommending movies and music on apps?
4. Which app uses AI for music recommendations?
5. What type of intelligence is used to control the temperature in a smart home?

Exercise 6- Answer the following questions in your own words.
1. How does AI make tasks more efficient in our everyday lives?
2. Give an example of how AI is used in smart home devices.
3. What is a virtual assistant, and how does it help people?
4. How does Siri improve its suggestions and help over time?
5. How does AI in video streaming platforms like Netflix help users find new shows to watch?

3.7 Project Work

Link:https://www.youtube.com/playlist?list=PLzlh_31VWEFoHuun1lUSRubhqr0LTnVUe

QR Code:

Exploring AI in everyday life

This is to help students understand how AI (Artificial Intelligence) is integrated into various aspects of everyday life, such as virtual assistants, entertainment, and smart home devices.

3.8 Group Discussion

Link:https://www.youtube.com/playlist?list=PLzlh_31VWEFpIgbQHBtLuCWj2-2Cx9qg6

QR Code:

How AI is used in everyday life

Students will discuss how AI is used in everyday life, such as smartphones, smart home devices, virtual assistants, and entertainment. They will explore how AI makes tasks like setting reminders, improving photos, and finding movies or music more accessible and personalised.

Discussion points:

What are some examples of AI that you use every day?
How does AI help make tasks more accessible at home or school?
Do you think AI is helpful, or are there any challenges or concerns?
How might AI continue to change the way we live in the future?

Link:https://www.youtube.com/playlist?list=PLzlh_31VWEFqu4Xeju o3ctJpq7PBvxkQ6

QR Code:

3.9 Case Study

AI super school

In a futuristic school, 12-year-old Arjun is amazed at how much AI is involved in his everyday learning. His classes feel like they are made just for him; the school's robots take care of all the tedious chores, and the AI can even predict when he's about to struggle with his homework. Arjun is curious: How do these systems work, and can they understand what he needs better than he does? He begins his adventure to discover the answers.

3.10 Fun Activity

Activity: AI scavenger hunt

Objective:

To engage students in understanding the practical applications of AI through fun and interactive activities.

Materials needed:

- Smartphones or tablets (optional)
- Printed scavenger hunt list
- Pens or pencils

Instructions:

Introduction to the activity:

Explain to the students that they will be going on an "AI Scavenger Hunt" to find examples of AI in their surroundings, either at home or in the classroom.

Create the scavenger hunt list:

Prepare a list of AI-related items or activities for the students to find. Examples:

- Find a device that uses a virtual assistant like Siri or Alexa.
- Spot a smart home device that controls temperature, lights, or security.
- Identify an app that recommends movies, music, or products on your phone.
- Locate a feature in your smartphone that uses AI to enhance photos.
- Identify a game that uses AI to control characters or opponents.
- If this is done at home, students can check with their parents to find these items.

The hunt:

- Give each student or group a scavenger hunt list.
- Students will have a set amount of time (e.g., 20-30 minutes) to find as many items as possible on the list.
- For each item found, students should write down what it is and how AI is used.

Sharing and discussion:

- After the scavenger hunt, gather the students to share what they found.
- Discuss how each AI example they found works and why it's useful.
- Ask students to think about other places or devices where they might discover AI in action.

Chapter-3

TEST PAPER
AI in Daily Life

Time Duration: 30 Minutes
Maximum Marks: 20

General Instructions:
1. This paper consists of twelve questions and is divided into two sections: A and B.
2. All questions are compulsory.
3. Section A comprises MCQs, Fill in the blanks, True or False, and One word of one mark each.
4. Section B comprises answer the following questions with three marks each.

SECTION-A

I - Choose the correct answer from the given options. **(1 X 2 = 2 marks)**

1. What is a virtual assistant?
   a) An intelligent computer program that helps you with different tasks
   b) A physical robot that cleans your house
   c) A video game character
   d) A calculator

2. Which company developed Siri?
   a) Amazon
   b) Google
   c) Apple
   d) Microsoft

II - Fill the blank space with the correct word. **(1 X 2 = 2 marks)**
1. AI can help in __________ languages instantly, making it easier to communicate with people who speak different languages.
2. In online shopping, AI helps by __________ products that you might like based on your previous searches and purchases.

III - Check if the sentence is true or false. **(1 X 2 = 2 marks)**
1. Siri is a virtual assistant developed by Amazon.
2. Virtual assistants can help with tasks like setting reminders and playing music.

IV - Write the answer in one word. **(1 X 2 = 2 marks)**
1. What do you call the AI feature that helps translate languages instantly?
2. What is the term for AI suggesting products based on your shopping habits?

SECTION-B

V - Answer the following questions in your own words. **(3 X 4 = 12 marks)**
1. How does AI assist in creating realistic animations in movies?
2. Explain how AI helps in diagnosing diseases in the medical field.
3. What role does AI play in video games to enhance the gaming experience?
4. In what way does AI contribute to improving navigation and finding routes in real time?

Answer

Exercise 1- 1. a) 2. b) 3. b) 4. b) 5. a)
Exercise 2- 1. False 2. True 3. False 4. True 5. False
Exercise 3- 1. convenience 2. AI 3. roads 4. Siri 5. Amazon
Exercise 4- 1. Siri 2. Alexa 3. Thermostat 4. Navigation 5. Personal
Exercise 5- 1. Siri 2. Self-driving 3. AI 4. Spotify 5. AI

Online Resources

Online Exam Paper Link:
Link: https://forms.gle/BeCjzCnwMyscLq2q9
QR Code:

Chapter 3 Videos Link:
Link: https://www.youtube.com/playlist?list=PLzlh_31VWEFpe_kZBmjnQxMy7kO_G09yM
QR Code:

More Sample Test Paper

Chapter 3 Test Paper – 1 Link:
Link: https://forms.gle/zuowsCakztnB92d47
QR Code:

Chapter 3 Test Paper – 2 Link:
Link: https://forms.gle/mCisXKM13MR1UJZq9
QR Code:

Chapter 3 Test Paper – 3 Link:
Link: https://forms.gle/haqX4tC66ATCJmJJ6
QR Code:

Chapter 3 Test Paper – 4 Link:
Link: https://forms.gle/3ftKPJj9PFTEVFQy5
QR Code:

HALF-YEARLY TEST PAPER

Time Duration: 90 Minutes
Maximum Marks: 40

General Instructions:
1. This paper consists of thirty questions and is divided into two sections: A and B.
2. All questions are compulsory.
3. Section A comprises MCQs. Fill in the blanks, True or False, Match the columns, and One-word questions with one mark each.
4. Section B comprises answers the following questions, each carrying three marks.

SECTION-A

I - Choose the correct answer from the given options. **(1 X 5 = 5 marks)**

1. Which of the following is NOT an example of AI?
a) Siri
b) Self-driving cars
c) Manual typewriter
d) Google Translate

2. AI helps in improving the quality of photos by:
a) Changing the phone's colour
b) Adjusting lighting and focus automatically
c) Enlarging the screen
d) Playing background music

3. Virtual assistants like Alexa can:
a) Control home devices
b) Print documents
c) Draw pictures
d) Repair cars

4. Which type of intelligence involves understanding and managing emotions?
a) Logical Intelligence
b) Emotional Intelligence
c) Musical Intelligence
d) Physical Intelligence

5. AI in video games is used to:
a) Control the game console
b) Manage game settings
c) Control non-player characters (NPCs)
d) Save game progress

II - Fill the blank space with the correct word. **(1 X 5 = 5 marks)**

1. AI can help __________ tasks that usually require Human Intelligence.
2. __________ Intelligence involves the ability to solve problems using logic.
3. AI can assist in finding the __________ route by analysing traffic conditions.
4. Virtual assistants can __________ your voice commands to perform tasks.
5. In AI, __________ refers to a machine's ability to improve its performance over time.

III - Check if the sentence is true or false. **(1 X 5 = 5 marks)**

1. AI is only helpful in video games and entertainment.
2. Machines can learn from data and adapt their behaviour accordingly.
3. Virtual assistants like Siri can control smart home devices.
4. Emotional intelligence is about solving math problems quickly.

5. AI can only be used in computers, not in smartphones.

IV - Match each word or phrase in Column A with Column B. **(1 X 5 = 5 marks)**

Column A	Column B
1. Siri	a) Learning from experience
2. Autonomous driving	b) Recommending products based on previous purchases
3. Learning	c) Virtual assistant developed by Apple
4. Recommendations	d) AI controlling cars without human intervention
5. Photo enhancement	e) Adjusting lighting and focus for better photo quality

V - Write the Answer in One Word. **(1 X 5 = 5 marks)**

1. What AI feature adjusts lighting and focus in smartphone cameras?
2. What term is used for AI's ability to learn from experience?
3. What do you call the AI technology used in self-driving cars?
4. What is the AI feature that provides product suggestions in online shopping?
5. What is the term for AI that understands and responds to voice commands?

SECTION-B

VI - Answer the following questions in your own words. **(3 X 5 = 15 marks)**

1. Describe how AI helps in online shopping.
2. How does AI improve the experience of using virtual assistants like Siri and Alexa?
3. Explain the concept of human intelligence and its importance.
4. What role does AI play in entertainment, specifically video streaming and gaming?
5. Why is learning considered an essential feature of AI?

More Online Sample Half-Yearly Test Paper

Half-yearly Test Paper – 1 Link:
Link: https://forms.gle/aqa4GRGntBnKAEYY6
QR Code:

Half-yearly Test Paper – 2 Link:
Link: https://forms.gle/bU9WsKjef1EfkYXc8
QR Code:

Half-yearly Test Paper – 3 Link:
Link: https://forms.gle/1uXAGCueWtfWhoZn9
QR Code:

Half-yearly Test Paper – 4 Link:
Link: https://forms.gle/qEYSEPxEmB7bLijv6
QR Code:

Chapter 4: Ethics in AI

Learning Objectives

Ethical Considerations in AI Development
Impact of AI on Jobs and Privacy
Myths vs. Facts about AI
Challenges in AI Ethics
Promoting Ethics in AI

4.1 Introduction to Ethics in Artificial Intelligence (AI)

Ethics is all about knowing what is right and what is wrong. When we discuss AI ethics, we ensure that AI is used in good and fair ways for everyone.

For example, if an AI system decides who gets a job, ethics ensure that the decision is fair and doesn't favour one person over another unfairly. Ethics also help protect people's personal information, like ensuring that an AI doesn't share your data without your permission.

In simple terms, ethics in AI are rules that ensure AI is used in a way that helps everyone and doesn't cause harm. It's about ensuring AI is safe, fair, and respectful of everyone's rights.

4.2 Ethical Considerations in AI Development

When developing AI, it's important to consider how it will affect people and the world around us. Here are some key ethical considerations that help ensure AI is used responsibly:

Fairness

Fairness means treating everyone equally. When we create AI, we must ensure it doesn't favour one person over another based on race, gender, or where they come from. For example, if an AI system chooses students for a particular program, it should give everyone an equal chance, no matter who they are.

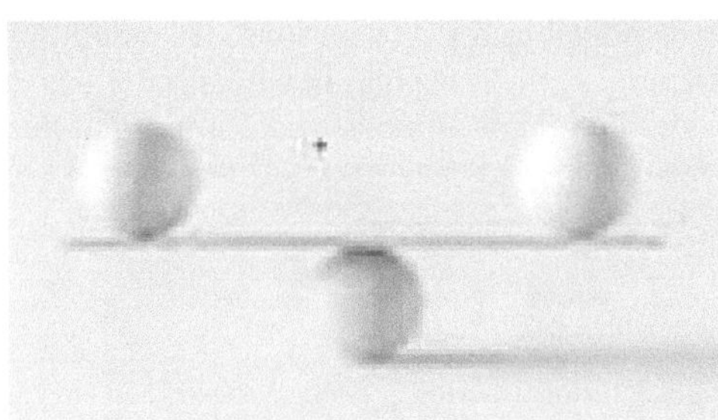

Transparency

Transparency means being open and transparent about how AI works. We should be able to understand how AI makes decisions. If an AI makes a choice, like selecting which job applicant to hire, we should be able to know why it made that choice. This helps people trust AI because they can see that it's working somewhat.

Privacy

Privacy is about protecting people's personal information. AI systems often use data to make decisions, but keeping this data safe is essential. AI should not use or share your personal information, like your name, address, or what you do online, without your permission. This helps keep your information safe and private.

Safety

Safety means ensuring AI doesn't harm people. Just like we ensure cars are safe to drive, we must ensure AI is safe to use. For example, if AI is used in a self-driving car, it should be carefully tested to ensure it doesn't cause accidents. Safety is crucial because we want AI to help people, not hurt them.

Accountability

Accountability means that someone is responsible for AI's actions. If something goes wrong with AI, there should be a person or a team who can fix it. For example, if an AI system in a hospital gives the wrong medical advice, doctors should be able to step in and correct it. AI should not be left alone to make important decisions without involving humans.

4.3 Impact of AI on jobs and privacy

AI is changing many things in our world, including how we work and how our personal information is handled. Here's how AI can impact jobs and privacy:

Impact on jobs

Job changes

AI can do some tasks that people usually do, like sorting mail, checking products in a factory, or even answering customer questions. This can mean that some jobs may change or disappear because machines do the work instead.

New job opportunities

While AI might take over some tasks, it also creates new jobs. For example, someone needs to design, build, and maintain AI systems. These new jobs might require learning new skills but can be exciting and offer new opportunities.

Helping people at work

AI can also help people do their jobs better. For example, AI can help doctors quickly analyse medical data to find the best patient treatment. In this way, AI can work alongside people, making their jobs more accessible and efficient.

Impact on privacy

Data collection

AI often needs a lot of information, or data, to work well. This data can include what you search for online, what videos you watch, or even where you go. This information helps AI learn and make decisions, like recommending a movie you might like.

Protecting personal information

The information AI collects must be kept safe. Privacy means ensuring that your details, like your name or where you live, aren't shared without your permission. For example, when you use an app that tracks your steps, the data should be protected so only you can see it.

Responsible use of Data

AI should be used responsibly to respect people's privacy. Companies and developers must ensure that AI systems don't misuse or mishandle your data. They should only collect the information they need and keep it secure.

4.4 Myths vs. Facts about AI

People discuss many ideas about AI, but not all of them are true. Let's look at some common myths about AI and the real facts.

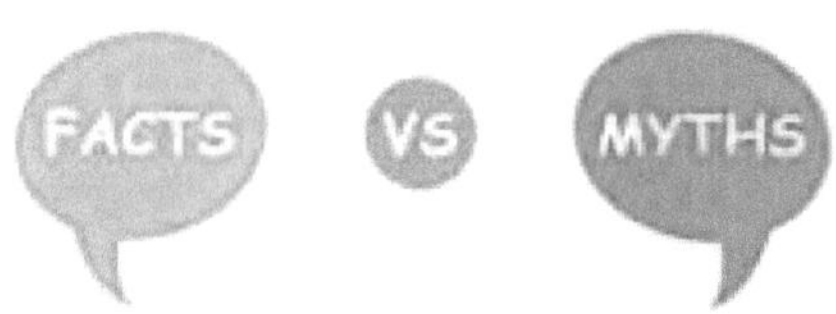

Myth 1: AI will take over all human jobs.
Fact:
AI can do some tasks but won't replace all human jobs. Instead, AI will likely take over repetitive or simple tasks, leaving people to focus on more creative and complex work. AI can also create new jobs that didn't exist before.

Myth 2: AI is smarter than humans.
Fact:
AI can be very good at specific tasks, like playing chess or solving math problems, but it doesn't have common sense or emotions like humans. AI can process information quickly but doesn't understand things like people do.

Myth 3: AI can make decisions without any mistakes.
Fact:
AI can make mistakes, just like humans. AI systems learn from Data; if the Data has errors or biases, the AI might make wrong decisions. That's why it's essential to check AI's decisions carefully.

Myth 4: AI is entirely independent and doesn't need human help.
Fact:
AI still needs humans to create, train, and monitor it. While AI can do many things independently, it relies on people to guide it, fix problems, and ensure its correct operation.

Myth 5: AI can do anything a human can do.

Fact:
AI is powerful, but it has limits. It's excellent at doing specific tasks like recognising faces or translating languages, but it can't do everything humans can, like showing emotions, being creative, or understanding complex human experiences.

Understanding the facts about AI helps us see what it can do and where its limits are. Knowing the truth is essential so we can use AI in the best way possible and not be misled by myths.

4.5 Challenges in AI Ethics

As AI becomes a part of our lives, it brings up some critical challenges that we must consider carefully. Here are some of the main difficulties in AI ethics:

Bias in AI
AI systems learn from Data, which sometimes has biases or unfair patterns. If the Data used to train AI is biased, the AI might make unjust decisions. For example, if an AI is trained with Data that favour one group of people over another, it might mistreat those groups. It's essential to ensure AI is trained with fair and balanced data.

Privacy concerns
AI often needs a lot of information about people to work well, which raises questions about privacy. How much personal information should AI be allowed to use? Protecting people's privacy means ensuring that AI only uses the Data it needs and keeps it safe from misuse.

Job displacement
As AI takes over some tasks people used to do, it might lead to job losses. While AI can make some jobs more accessible, it can also replace specific jobs, which might be difficult for people who rely on them. Finding ways to help people learn new skills and employment is a significant challenge.

Security risks
AI systems can be targets for hackers or people who want to misuse them. For example, if someone hacks into an AI system used in a self-driving car, it could cause serious harm. Keeping AI systems secure and protected from attacks is a big challenge.

Lack of transparency
Sometimes, it's hard to understand how AI makes decisions. This lack of transparency can make it challenging to trust AI systems, mainly when used in critical areas like healthcare or law. We need to ensure AI is clear and understandable so people can trust its decisions.

Accountability
If something goes wrong with AI, like if it makes a mistake or causes harm, it can be unclear who is responsible. Is it the person who made the AI, the person who used it, or the AI itself? Ensuring that there is accountability, or someone who can be held responsible, is crucial.

These challenges in AI ethics show us that while AI has great potential, we must be careful and thoughtful in developing and using it. We can ensure that AI benefits everyone reasonably and safely by addressing these challenges.

4.6 Ethical AI in different industries

AI is used in various industries, each with its ethical considerations. Let's look at how AI ethics play a role in some key areas:

1. Healthcare

AI in diagnosis: AI is used to help doctors diagnose diseases by analysing medical images or patient data. However, ethical concerns arise when AI systems make mistakes, potentially leading to incorrect diagnoses.

Patient privacy: AI systems must protect the sensitive health information they use. Ethical AI in healthcare ensures that patient data is kept confidential and secure.
Bias in treatment: AI should provide fair and unbiased treatment recommendations. For instance, AI should not favour one group of patients over another based-on race, gender, or other factors.

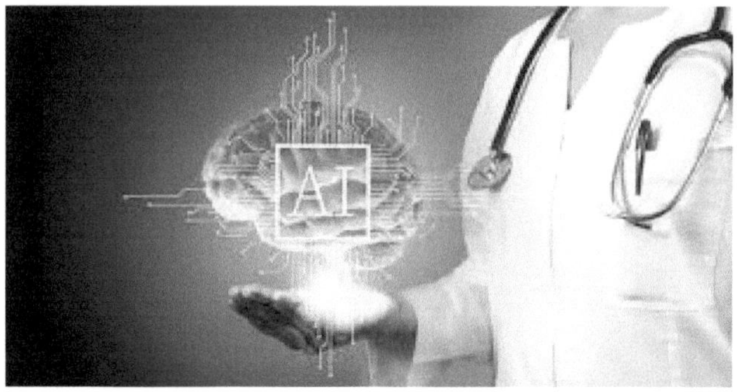

2. Education

Personalised learning: AI can help create personalised learning experiences for students. However, these systems mustn't unfairly disadvantage students from different backgrounds.
Data privacy: Schools using AI must keep student data private and secure, protecting students' rights.
Fair access: Ethical AI in education should be accessible to all students, regardless of their economic background, ensuring everyone has equal opportunities to benefit from AI.

3. Finance

AI in banking: AI detects fraud and manages investments. However, if AI systems are biased, they could unfairly deny loans or financial services to specific groups.
Transparency: In finance, it's crucial that AI decisions, like credit approvals, are transparent so that customers understand why they were accepted or denied.
Security: AI systems in finance must be secure to protect sensitive financial data from being stolen or misused.

4.7 Real-Life Case Studies of Ethical AI

Examining real-life examples of how AI ethics are applied can help students understand the importance of these issues.

Case Study 1: Facial Recognition Technology

Facial recognition AI is used for security, such as unlocking phones or identifying people in public spaces. However, it raises ethical concerns about privacy and bias. For example, studies have shown that some facial recognition systems are less accurate at identifying people with darker skin tones. This bias can lead to unfair treatment, such as wrongful arrests.

Ethical Lessons:

Importance of fairness and accuracy in AI systems.

The need for transparency and accountability in AI development.

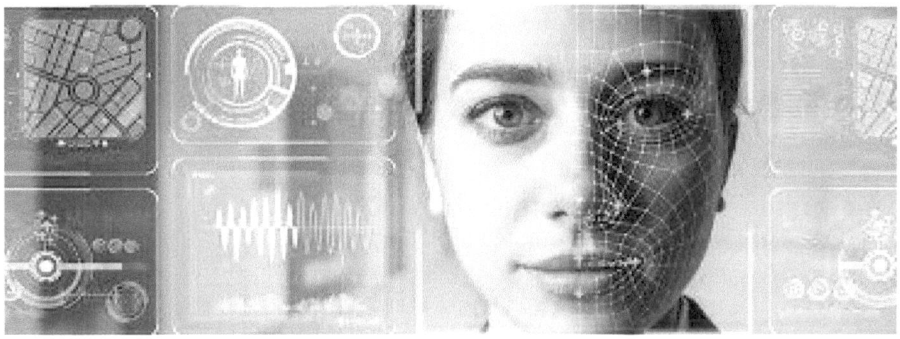

Case Study 2: AI in hiring

Some companies use AI to screen job applicants by analysing resumes and conducting initial interviews. However, if the AI is trained on biased data, it might favour specific candidates over others, leading to unfair hiring practices.

Ethical lessons:

The importance of unbiased data in training AI systems.

Ensuring AI does not perpetuate existing inequalities.

Case Study 3: Autonomous vehicles

Self-driving cars use AI to navigate roads and avoid accidents. While they promise to reduce traffic accidents, ethical challenges arise when these cars must make split-second decisions, such as choosing between two potentially harmful outcomes.

Ethical lessons:

The complexity of programming AI to make ethical decisions in life-and-death situations.

There is a need for clear guidelines and regulations to ensure the safety and fairness of AI systems.

4.8 The Role of Governments and Organizations in AI Ethics

Governments and organisations worldwide play a crucial role in promoting ethical AI. Here's how they contribute:

Government Regulations

Laws and Policies: Governments can create rules that regulate the use of AI, ensuring it is used ethically. For example, regulations can require companies to be transparent about using AI and protect citizens' privacy.

Ethical AI committees: Some governments establish committees to study AI ethics and make recommendations. These committees can help guide the development of AI policies and standards.

International Cooperation

Global standards: AI is used worldwide, so international cooperation is needed to create global standards for ethical AI. Countries can work together to ensure AI is used responsibly and benefits everyone.

Sharing knowledge: Countries and organisations can share knowledge and best practices on AI ethics, helping each other address ethical challenges.

Corporate Responsibility

Ethical AI Development: Companies developing AI should follow ethical guidelines to ensure their products are fair, transparent, and safe. This includes testing AI systems for bias and ensuring they respect privacy.

Corporate Social Responsibility: Companies can contribute to AI ethics by supporting initiatives that promote fairness, diversity, and inclusion in AI development.

4.9 The Future of Ethical AI

As AI technology continues to advance, the ethical considerations will evolve. Here's what the future might hold:

AI and Human Rights

Protecting Rights: As AI becomes more integrated into society, it will be crucial to protect human rights. AI should be developed and used to respect individual freedoms and promote equality.

Empowering people: AI can empower people, giving them more control over their lives and access to opportunities. Ethical AI should focus on improving the quality of life for everyone.

Ethical AI in Space Exploration

AI in space: AI is used in space exploration to navigate spacecraft and analyse data. Ethical considerations in this field include ensuring that AI systems are reliable and that space exploration benefits all of humanity, not just a few countries or companies.

AI and the environment

Sustainable AI: The development of AI should be environmentally sustainable. This means using energy-efficient technologies and ensuring that AI is used to address environmental challenges, such as climate change.

Ethical Impact: AI can help monitor and protect the environment, but it's essential to ensure that its use doesn't harm ecosystems or contribute to pollution.

4.10 Promoting Ethics in AI

To make sure AI is used in ways that are fair, safe, and good for everyone, we need to promote ethics in AI. Here are some ways to do that:

Education
One of the best ways to promote ethics in AI is through education. This means teaching people, including students like you, about using AI responsibly. By learning about AI and its impact, we can make better decisions about how to use it.

Laws and Regulations
Governments can create rules and laws to ensure that AI is used ethically. These rules can help protect people's rights, ensure fairness, and ensure that AI systems are safe. For example, laws could require AI to protect personal information or be transparent about how it makes decisions.

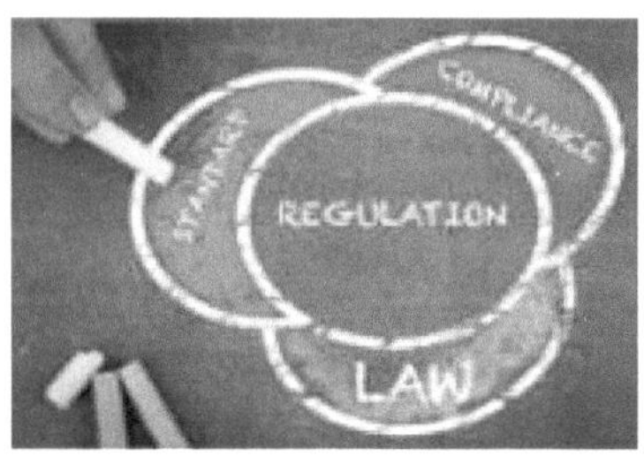

Collaboration
Promoting ethics in AI also means working together. Scientists, engineers, teachers, and even students can collaborate to ensure AI is developed in a way that benefits everyone. When different people share ideas and collaborate, they can find the best ways for AI responsible.

Raising awareness
It's important to talk about the ethical challenges of AI so that more people are aware of them. By discussing these issues, we can help others understand the importance of ethics in AI. This can lead to better practices and more responsible use of AI daily.

Responsible AI Development

When creating AI systems, developers should always consider ethics. This means considering how the AI will impact people, ensuring it's fair, and respecting privacy and safety. Developers should be open about how their AI works and make it easy for others to understand.

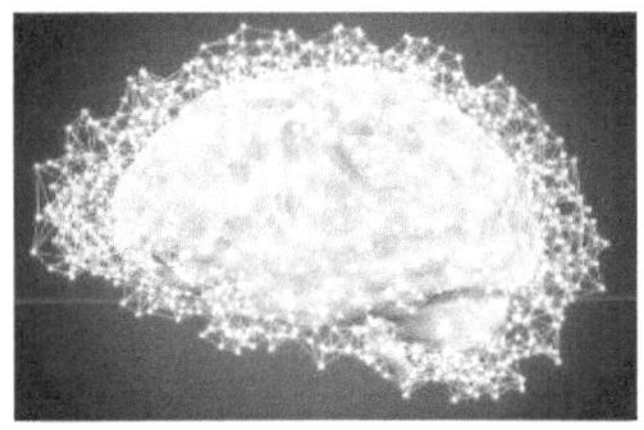

By promoting ethics in AI through education, laws, collaboration, awareness, and responsible development, we can ensure AI is used in ways that help people and avoid causing harm. This way, AI can be a positive force that benefits everyone.

4.11 Summary

Ethics in AI ensures that AI is used fairly, safely and respects people's rights.
Key ethical considerations include fairness, transparency, privacy, safety, and accountability.
Promoting ethics in AI involves education, laws, collaboration, and responsible development.
Ethical AI can be promoted through education, guidelines, involving diverse perspectives, and continuous monitoring and improvement.
Ethical AI in Industries: Different industries, like healthcare, education, and finance, face unique ethical challenges with AI, including fairness, privacy, and security concerns.
Real-Life Case Studies: Examples like facial recognition, AI in hiring, and autonomous vehicles highlight the importance of addressing bias, transparency, and safety in AI.
Role of Governments and Organizations: Governments and organisations can promote ethical AI through regulations, international cooperation, and corporate responsibility.

4.12 Glossary

Ethics: Principles of right and wrong guiding actions and decisions.
Fairness: Treating everyone equally.
Transparency: Being open about how decisions are made.
Privacy: Protecting personal information from misuse.
Bias: A prejudice in AI systems that can lead to unfair treatment of individuals or groups.
Data Collection: Gathering information for AI systems to analyse and learn from.
Facial Recognition Technology: AI technology that identifies or verifies individuals based on facial features is often used in security.
Autonomous vehicles: Self-driving cars that use AI to navigate and make driving decisions without human input.
Regulations: Rules and laws set by governments to control how AI is developed and used.
Corporate Social Responsibility: The ethical obligations of companies to ensure their AI technologies are fair, transparent, and safe.

Sustainable AI: AI development that is environmentally friendly and helps address global challenges like climate change.
Human Rights: The basic rights and freedoms that AI must respect and protect, ensuring fairness and equality for all people.

4.13 Exercise

Exercise 1 – Choose the correct answer from the given options.

1. What does fairness in AI mean?
   a) Giving everyone an equal chance
   b) Hiding how AI works
   c) Using personal data without permission
   d) Making mistakes without correction

2. What should AI developers focus on to ensure safety?
   a) Making AI systems look attractive
   b) Ensuring AI doesn't cause harm
   c) Collecting as much data as possible
   d) Hiding AI decisions from users

3. What is a common myth about AI?
   a) AI can replace all human jobs
   b) AI can help in specific tasks
   c) AI needs human help
   d) AI can make mistakes

4. Which of the following is a challenge in AI ethics?
   a) AI always being fair
   b) AI making decisions without bias
   c) AI systems being hacked
   d) AI being completely transparent

5. How can we promote ethics in AI?
   a) By ignoring how AI affects people
   b) Through education and laws
   c) By using AI without rules
   d) By keeping AI secret from everyone

Exercise 2 – Fill the blank space with the correct word.

1. ________ means treating everyone equally when using AI.
2. AI systems should protect people's ________ information.
3. A lack of ________ in AI can make it difficult to trust its decisions.
4. Education helps people understand the importance of using AI ________.
5. ________ means that someone is responsible for the actions of AI.

Exercise 3 – Match each word or phrase in Column A with Column B.

Column A	Column B
1. Fairness	a) Keeping data safe
2. Privacy	b) Treating everyone equally
3. Transparency	c) AI not causing harm
4. Safety	d) Understanding AI decisions
5. Accountability	e) Being responsible for AI

Exercise 4 – Read the questions below and find the appropriate word in the provided grid.

1. What is the principle that ensures AI treats everyone equally?
2. What is the term for protecting personal information in AI?

3. What does AI need to protect regarding personal information?
4. What must AI ensure to avoid causing harm?
5. What describes the challenge of AI learning from biased data?

S	E	C	U	R	I	T	Y
D	Y	Q	I	Q	R	U	J
E	C	S	Q	A	E	O	T
S	A	S	Z	T	L	V	N
A	V	E	B	L	N	R	Y
I	I	N	Z	P	M	D	X
B	R	R	Z	J	A	J	J
N	P	I	I	T	Y	P	H
U	H	A	A	F	T	T	N
U	C	F	N	Y	Y	O	J

Exercise 5 – Answer the following questions in your own words.

1. What does transparency in AI means?
2. Why is fairness important in AI?
3. How can AI impact jobs?
4. What is a common myth about AI?
5. Why is promoting ethics in AI important?

Exercise 6 - Decode the secret message by solving the puzzles below. Each correct answer gives you a letter. Combine them to reveal the final AI-related word or phrase.

Math puzzle	Solve this simple math problem: "What is 4 + 1?" The answer corresponds to the 5th letter in the alphabet. What letter is it? (Use the letter for final answer)	....
Word scramble	Unscramble the following letters to form a word related to AI: "POLEVED" (Use the first letter for final answer)	....
Riddle	I am the process by which software and technology are created. What am I? (Use the letter for final answer)	....
Math puzzle	Solve this math problem to find the corresponding letter: "What is 15 - 2?" (Use the letter for final answer)	....
Final clue	Combine the letters you've found in each puzzle to reveal the final AI-related word or phrase. (Use the letters from the puzzles above, then add "O" and "P" to complete the word)	....

4.14 Project Work

Link: https://www.youtube.com/playlist?list=PLzlh_31VWEFoUpWmTknbEn6EL-DSPPM5o

QR Code:

AI Ethics comic strip

This project aims to help students understand AI ethics by creating a comic strip that tells a story about how AI should be used responsibly.

4.15 Group Discussion

Link: https://www.youtube.com/playlist?list=PLzlh_31VWEFpJ2UFvQTgCjfUNe8z4argN

QR Code:

AI Ethics treasure hunt

Learn about AI ethics through a fun, interactive treasure hunt.

Instructions:

1. The teacher hides cards around the classroom with different ethical challenges related to AI (e.g., "The AI took my data without asking!").
2. Each card also includes a clue leading to the next hidden card.
3. Students find all the cards in pairs or small groups.
4. Once all the cards are found, students discuss how to solve each ethical problem.
5. The first group to complete the hunt and develop reasonable solutions wins a small prize!

4.16 Case Study

Link: https://www.youtube.com/playlist?list=PLzlh_31VWEFpDEgyXhYsG7-wYPT3sfzJ4

QR Code:

Has AI shopping assistance gone too far?

ShopSmart launched an AI shopping assistant that suggests products based on browsing history and social media activity. Riya, a 12-year-old user, notices the AI only recommends the same types of products and feels the recommendations are biased. Additionally, she received a product offer based on a private conversation with her family, raising concerns about her privacy.

4.17 Fun Activity

Activity: AI Ethics role-play relay

Objective:

Students will explore AI ethics through a role-play relay, acting out scenarios and making quick decisions about how AI should behave.

Materials needed:

Scenario Cards, Role-Play Props (Optional), Station Signs, Solution Sheets, Timer/Stopwatch, Fun Badges/Stickers, Classroom Space and Whiteboard/Chalkboard.

Instructions:

1. Set up the relay:

The classroom is divided into 3-4 stations. Each station represents a different ethical scenario involving AI.

At each station, a card describes the scenario and provides the students' roles (e.g., AI system, user, and affected person).

2. Form teams:

Students are divided into teams of 4-5. Each team will rotate through the stations, acting out the scenarios and solving the ethical dilemmas presented.

3. Role-play at each station:

Station 1: Fairness dilemma

Scenario: An AI assigns resources (like books or tablets) to students, but it's giving more to some students than others.

Roles: AI, Student receiving more, Student receiving less, teacher, etc.

Task: The team must act out the scenario and decide how to make the AI fairer.

Station 2: Privacy concern

Scenario: An AI assistant collects Data from students without asking for permission.

Roles: AI, concerned students and parents.

Task: The team discusses and role-plays how the AI should handle Data more responsibly.

Station 3: Safety issue

Scenario: An AI robot moves too quickly in the school hallway, almost causing accidents.

Roles: AI robot, student and teacher.

Task: The team acts out the situation and decides how to make the robot safer.

Station 4: Transparency problem

Scenario: An AI makes decisions about grades, but students don't know how it calculates them.

Roles: AI, student and teacher.

Task: The team role-plays how to make the AI more transparent and understandable.

4. Quick decision time:

After role-playing the scenario, the team has two minutes to discuss and write down a solution to the ethical problem. They should consider making AI fairer, safer, or more transparent.

5. Relay rotation:

After completing one station, the teams rotate to the next station until all stations are completed. Each station introduces a new ethical challenge.

6. Debrief and share:

Once all teams have completed the relay, they gather to share their solutions with the class. The teacher leads a discussion on the different approaches and highlights the importance of ethics in AI.

7. Award fun badges:

Based on their solutions, teams can receive fun badges like "Fairness Champion", "Privacy Protector", or "Safety Star". This adds an element of friendly competition and reinforces learning.

6 Effective Ways

TO STUDY BETTER

1 EFFECTIVE PLANNING

Create a study schedule that breaks down your tasks into manageable sessions, ensuring a balance between subjects and topics

2 ACTIVE LEARNING

Engage actively with the material through methods like summarizing information, teaching concepts to others, and participating in discussions.

3 VARIED STUDY METHODS

Utilize different study techniques, such as reading, note-taking, flashcards, and practice questions, to reinforce learning through various approaches.

4 HEALTHY ENVIRONMENT

Choose a comfortable and well-lit study environment, minimizing distractions to enhance focus and concentration.

5 REGULAR BREAKS

Take short breaks during study sessions to prevent mental fatigue and maintain overall productivity.

6 SELF-ASSESSMENT

Regularly evaluate your understanding of the material through self-assessment tools, quizzes, or practice exams to identify areas that need further review.

Chapter-4

TEST PAPER
Ethics in AI

Time Duration: 30 Minutes
Maximum Marks: 20

General Instructions:
1. This paper consists of twelve questions and is divided into two sections: A and B.
2. All questions are compulsory.
3. Section A comprises MCQs, Fill in the blanks, True or False, and One word of one mark each.
4. Section B comprises answer the following questions with three marks each.

SECTION-A

I - Choose the correct answer from the given options. **(1 X 2 = 2 marks)**

1. Which ethical consideration ensures that AI does not harm people?
   a) Transparency
   b) Safety
   c) Privacy
   d) Fairness

2. What must AI be so people can trust its decisions?
   a) Complicated
   b) Secretive
   c) Transparent
   d) Unfair

II - Fill the blank space with the correct word. **(1 X 2 = 2 marks)**

1. ________ in AI means that everyone is treated the same without any discrimination.
2. ________ systems can create new jobs as well as change existing ones.

III - Check if the sentence is true or false. **(1 X 2 = 2 marks)**

1. AI can operate independently without any human oversight.
2. Protecting personal data is an essential ethical consideration in AI.

IV - Write the answer in one word. **(1 X 2 = 2 marks)**

1. What term describes making sure AI decisions are open and transparent?
2. What ethical principle focuses on not causing harm through AI?

SECTION-B

V - Answer the following questions in your own words. **(3 X 4 = 12 marks)**

1. Why is accountability necessary in AI?
2. How does AI impact privacy?
3. What is one challenge related to bias in AI?
4. Why should AI developers consider ethics in their work?

Answer

Exercise 1- 1. a) 2. b) 3. a) 4. c) 5. b)
Exercise 2- 1. fairness 2. personal 3. transparency 4. responsibly 5. accountability
Exercise 3- 1. b) 2. a) 3. d) 4. c) 5. e)
Exercise 4- 1. Fairness 2. Privacy 3. Data 4. Security 5. Unbiased

Online Resources

Online Exam Paper Link:
Link: https://forms.gle/ZQE3LSsVWkaKgKyM7
QR Code:

Chapter 4 Videos Link:
Link: https://www.youtube.com/playlist?list=PLzlh_31VWEFpLoD0oi4NVOLnGHvCjf2Vz
QR Code:

More Sample Test Paper

Chapter 4 Test Paper – 1 Link:
Link: https://forms.gle/QvMpuudpExJeXCq9A
QR Code:

Chapter 4 Test Paper – 2 Link:
Link: https://forms.gle/MTnfwrAU9MZiT2VLA
QR Code:

Chapter 4 Test Paper – 3 Link:
Link: https://forms.gle/ch79eyLearJG5LBeA
QR Code:

Chapter 4 Test Paper – 4 Link:
Link: https://forms.gle/es8sDDao6dyZbdRj9
QR Code:

Chapter 5: Augmented & Virtual Reality

Learning Objectives

Introduction to AR and VR
Difference between AI and VR
Use of AR in Daily Lives
Computer Vision
Applications of Computer Vision

5.1 Introduction to AR and VR

Two exciting concepts in technology are changing how we experience the world: Augmented Reality (AR) and Virtual Reality (VR). These technologies allow us to see and interact with digital objects in new ways. In this chapter, we will explore what AR and VR are, how they work, and how they are used in our daily lives.

What is Augmented Reality (AR)?

Augmented Reality (AR) is a technology that overlays digital information—such as images, sounds, or other data—onto the real world. This means you can see and interact with digital objects while being aware of your surroundings. Imagine using your smartphone camera to view your classroom. With AR, you might see virtual animals walking around your classroom or arrows pointing to different objects, providing information about them. The real world is still there, but it's enhanced with these digital additions.

Examples of Augmented Reality (AR):

AR Games: Games like Pokémon GO use AR to place virtual characters in real-world environments. You can see Pokémon on your phone screen when you play as if they were right before you.

AR in Education: AR apps can bring textbooks to life by showing 3D models, animations, and additional information when you point your device at a page.

AR in Shopping: Some apps let you use AR to see how furniture or decorations will look in your home before you buy them. You can point your phone at a spot in your room, and the app will show a virtual version of the item in place.

How does Augmented Reality (AR) work?

AR uses a device like a smartphone or tablet camera to capture the real world. Then, it uses software to add digital objects to the scene. This could be anything from a virtual character to a piece of information. The device's screen combines the natural world and digital objects, creating an augmented experience.

What is Virtual Reality (VR)?

Virtual Reality (VR) is a technology that creates a completely immersive digital environment. When you put on a VR headset, you are taken into a virtual world that feels real, even though it's entirely computer-generated. Everything you see and hear in VR is part of this digital world; you can interact with it just like in the real world.

When you wear a VR headset, you might find yourself exploring an underwater world, flying through space, or playing inside a video game. In VR, the real world is replaced by this digital environment, and you feel like you're genuinely there.

Examples of VR:

VR games: In VR games, you can explore virtual worlds, interact with objects, and even feel like you are part of the action. For example, you might play a game where you explore space, fly a spaceship, or fight virtual enemies.

VR in education: VR can take virtual field trips to places like ancient Egypt or outer space. You can explore these environments as if you were there.

VR in training: Professionals like pilots, doctors, and firefighters use VR to practice their skills in a safe, controlled environment. For example, a pilot can practice flying in a virtual aeroplane before taking off in a real one.

How VR works:

VR uses a headset with screens in front of your eyes to create the illusion of being in a different place. The headset tracks your head movements, so when you look around, the virtual environment moves with you, making it feel like you are there. VR can also use hand controllers to let you interact with virtual objects, like picking up a ball or opening a virtual door.

AR and VR are becoming more popular in games, education, and even shopping, making these activities more fun and interactive. While AR adds to the real world, VR creates a new world to explore.

5.2 The History and Evolution of AR and VR

Understanding AR and VR technologies' origins and evolution over time is essential for fully appreciating them.

Early beginnings

Stereoscopic viewers (1838): Creating a three-dimensional (3D) experience began in the 19th century with the invention of stereoscopic viewers. These devices used two slightly different images viewed through lenses to create a 3D effect, which laid the groundwork for future virtual experiences.

The Sensorama (1962): Morton Heilig invented the Sensorama, one of the earliest attempts at creating a virtual reality experience. The Sensorama machine combined 3D video with smells, vibrations, and sounds to create an immersive experience. Although it wasn't interactive, it was a precursor to modern VR.

Development of AR and VR Technologies

Virtual Reality in the 1960s and 70s: The idea of VR started to take shape with the development of the first head-mounted displays (HMDs) in the 1960s. A computer scientist, Ivan Sutherland created the "Sword of Damocles," the first HMD that displayed basic computer graphics. However, it was heavy and required a lot of equipment to operate.

Early Augmented Reality (1990s): Tom Caudell coined the term "Augmented Reality" in the 1990s while working at Boeing. He used AR to help workers visualise how to assemble aircraft parts by overlaying digital instructions onto real-world components.

Gaming and consumer interest (1990s): The 1990s saw the first commercial attempts to bring VR to consumers, particularly in gaming. Companies like Sega and Nintendo released VR headsets, but they were limited by the technology of the time, offering low-quality graphics and a poor user experience.

Modern advancements

Smartphones and AR (2008-2010s): The introduction of smartphones with advanced cameras, sensors, and processing power enabled the development of AR apps. Apps like Snapchat and Pokémon GO brought AR into the mainstream by allowing users to interact with virtual objects overlaid on the natural world through their phones.

Consumer VR (2010s-present): The 2010s saw a resurgence in VR with the development of more affordable and powerful VR headsets like the Oculus Rift, HTC Vive, and PlayStation VR. These devices provided high-quality VR experiences, making the technology more accessible to consumers.

Mixed Reality (MR): In addition to AR and VR, a new technology called Mixed Reality (MR) emerged. MR combines elements of both AR and VR, allowing natural and virtual objects to interact with each other in real-time. Microsoft's HoloLens is one example of an MR device that overlays holographic images onto the natural world and lets users interact with them.

5.3 Difference Between AI and VR

Artificial Intelligence (AI) and Virtual Reality (VR) are essential technologies with different roles and uses. Let's understand the difference between them:

Aspect	Artificial Intelligence (AI)	Virtual Reality (VR)
Definition	AI is like the brain of a machine, enabling computers to think, learn, and make decisions.	VR creates an entirely new and immersive digital environment.
Function	Allows computers to analyse data, recognise patterns, and solve problems like humans.	It places users into an authentic digital world, even though it's entirely computer-generated.
Purpose	It makes machines intelligent enough to perform tasks requiring human-like thought.	Creates an immersive experience where users can interact with a virtual environment.
Interaction	AI interacts with data and makes decisions based on that data.	VR allows users to interact with a virtual environment.
Application	Used in smart devices, data analysis, games, and more.	Used in gaming, education, training, and simulations.
Hardware	Runs on computers, smartphones, and other smart devices.	Requires VR headsets and controllers.

They serve different purposes but can be combined to create even more advanced technologies.

5.4 The Science Behind AR and VR

Let's examine the basic science and technology behind AR and VR to understand better how they work.

The Technology of Augmented Reality (AR)

Cameras and sensors: AR relies on cameras and sensors to capture the real-world environment. The camera on your smartphone or tablet acts as the AR system's eyes, capturing everything around you.

Processing power: Once the real-world environment is captured, the device's processor analyses the data to identify surfaces, objects, and the context in which digital elements should be placed. This analysis happens in real time, so the digital elements appear instantly on your screen.

Graphics and display: The device then overlays digital graphics onto the real-world image captured by the camera. These graphics can be anything from simple text to complex 3D models, and they move and change as you move the device, maintaining the illusion that they are part of the real world.

Tracking and mapping: AR systems use advanced algorithms to track your movements and the camera's position. This allows digital objects to stay in place relative to the real world, even as you move around.

The Technology of Virtual Reality (VR)

VR headsets: A VR headset is the most important piece of equipment for experiencing VR. It has two small screens inside, one for each eye, that create a 3D image by displaying slightly different views of the virtual environment to each eye, just like how our eyes see the real world.

Motion tracking: VR headsets have sensors that track head movements. When you turn your head, the view in the VR world changes just as it would in the real world. Some VR systems also include hand controllers that track hand movement, allowing you to interact with objects in the virtual environment.

Sound and haptics: To make VR experiences even more immersive, many VR systems include headphones that provide 3D audio, making sounds come from the right direction as they would in the real world. Some advanced VR systems also use haptic feedback, which means the controllers or other devices vibrate or provide resistance, so you can "feel" virtual objects.

Rendering and simulation: The VR system's processor and graphics card work together to create the virtual environment. This involves rendering 3D graphics, simulating physics (like gravity and collision), and ensuring the experience runs smoothly without lag.

5.4 Benefits and Challenges of AR and VR

While AR and VR offer many exciting possibilities, they also have some challenges. Let's explore both the benefits and the obstacles of these technologies.

Benefits of AR and VR

Enhanced learning: AR and VR make learning more engaging and effective by providing interactive and immersive experiences. Students can explore historical sites, conduct virtual experiments, or travel inside the human body.

Improved training: VR can be used for safe, risk-free training by professionals in medicine, aviation, and the military. For example, surgeons can practice complex operations in a virtual environment before performing them on actual patients.

Creative expression: AR and VR provide new tools for artists, designers, and creators to express their ideas in never-before-possible ways. Virtual art galleries, 3D sculptures, and interactive storytelling are just a few examples.

Increased accessibility: VR can bring experiences to people who might not otherwise have access to them. For example, students in remote areas can use VR to visit museums or landmarks, and people with disabilities can experience places and activities that might be difficult in the real world.

Challenges of AR and VR

Technical limitations: Creating realistic and responsive AR and VR experiences requires advanced technology, which can be expensive and challenging to develop. Additionally, VR systems need powerful computers to run smoothly, which can be costly.

Motion sickness: Some people experience motion sickness when using VR, as the brain can become confused by the difference between what the eyes see and what the body feels. This is a common challenge that developers are working to minimise.

Privacy concerns: AR systems that use cameras to capture the real world can raise privacy concerns, as they might inadvertently record and store images or videos of people without their consent.

Physical safety: Because VR users are immersed in a virtual world, they might not be aware of their physical surroundings, leading to accidents like bumping into furniture or tripping over objects.

Ethical issues: As AR and VR become more widespread, ethical questions arise about how these technologies should be used. For example, how should VR content be regulated to prevent misuse, and how can AR ensure it doesn't create a distorted view of reality?

5.5 Use of AR in daily life

Augmented Reality (AR) is a technology that blends the digital world with the real world. It allows us to see and interact with virtual objects as part of our surroundings. Here are some ways AR is used in our daily lives:

Education

AR makes learning more fun and interactive. For example, with AR, students can point their tablets at a picture of the solar system and see the planets come to life in 3D, helping them understand concepts better.

Shopping
AR helps people shop smarter. Some apps allow you to see how furniture or decorations will look in your home before you buy them. This means you can ensure something fits and looks good before purchasing.

Entertainment
Games like Pokémon Go use AR to make the gaming experience more exciting. In these games, digital characters appear in the real world through your phone's camera, making it feel like you're catching Pokémon in your neighbourhood.

Navigation
AR can help with directions. Some navigation apps use AR to show arrows and signs on your phone screen that guide you to your destination, making it easier to follow directions.

Social media
AR is used in social media apps to add fun effects to your photos and videos. Filters that add bunny ears or change your background are examples of AR at work.

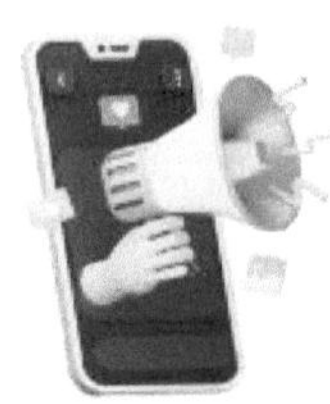

5.6 Ethical and Social Implications of AR and VR
As AR and VR technologies become more advanced and widespread, it's essential to consider their ethical and social implications.

Ethical Considerations

Privacy concerns: AR devices often rely on cameras and sensors to function, which can raise privacy concerns. For example, if AR glasses constantly record the environment, they could capture images or videos of people without their consent.

Data security: AR and VR systems collect large amounts of Data about their users, such as their movements, preferences, and interactions. Ensuring this Data is secure and used responsibly is a significant ethical challenge.

Digital addiction: As AR and VR experiences become more immersive and engaging, there is a risk that people might spend too much time in virtual environments, potentially leading to addiction or a disconnection from the real world.

Bias and representation: AR and VR content development needs to consider diversity and inclusivity. If virtual environments are not designed with everyone in mind, they could reinforce stereotypes or exclude certain groups of people.

Social Implications

Impact on social interaction: AR and VR can change how people interact with each other. While these technologies offer new ways to connect, such as virtual meetings and social spaces, they could also reduce face-to-face interactions, leading to potential social isolation.

Access and equality: Not everyone can access the latest AR and VR technologies due to cost, availability, or other barriers. Ensuring that these technologies are accessible to all, regardless of socioeconomic status, is essential for promoting equality.

Influence on perception: AR and VR can shape how people perceive reality. For example, AR could be used to create convincing advertisements or alter a person's perception of their surroundings. It is important to consider how these technologies might influence beliefs, opinions, and decisions.

5.7 Computer Vision

Computer Vision is a branch of Artificial Intelligence (AI) that enables machines to "see" and understand the visual world, just like humans do. It's like giving a computer eyes to recognise and interpret images, videos, and other visual information.

Imagine you take a picture of your pet dog. With computer vision, AI can analyse the picture and identify a dog, not a cat or a tree. This ability to recognise objects in images and videos makes computer vision so powerful.

Application of Computer Vision

Face Recognition

Face recognition technology unlocks smartphones and secures devices by recognising the user's face. The phone's camera captures an image of your face, and AI compares it to stored data to ensure it's you. This technology is also used in social media platforms to automatically tag friends in photos, making it easier to organise and share memories.

Healthcare

In healthcare, computer vision assists doctors in analyzing medical images like X-rays, MRIs, and CT scans. AI can identify patterns and abnormalities that might be challenging for the human eye to spot, such as early indicators of diseases like cancer. This technology supports quicker and more accurate diagnoses, enhancing patient care and outcomes.

Self-Driving cars

Computer vision is essential for self-driving cars, allowing them to "see" the road. The AI in these cars recognises traffic signs, pedestrians, other vehicles, and obstacles. It helps the car decide when to stop, turn, or slow down, ensuring a safe driving experience without human intervention.

5.8 Summary

AR enhances the real world with digital elements, while VR creates immersive virtual environments.
AI focuses on learning and decision-making, while VR creates new digital experiences.
AR is used in education, shopping, and entertainment.
Computer Vision is an AI technology that enables machines to see and understand images with face recognition, image search, and healthcare applications.

5.9 Glossary

Augmented Reality (AR): Technology that overlays digital content onto the real world.
Virtual Reality (VR): Technology that creates fully immersive virtual environments.
Face Recognition: AI technology that identifies and verifies individuals by analysing facial features.
Image search: A feature that allows finding information or products online using images instead of text.

5.10 Exercise

Exercise 1 – Choose the correct answer from the given options.

1. What does Augmented Reality (AR) do?
   a) Creates a fully immersive digital environment
   b) Enhances the real world with digital elements
   c) Teaches computers to think like humans
   d) Makes virtual worlds for gaming

2. Which of the following technologies requires a headset to use?
   a) Augmented Reality
   b) Virtual Reality
   c) Face Recognition
   d) Computer Vision

3. What is the primary function of Computer Vision?
   a) To create virtual environments
   b) To recognize and interpret visual information
   c) To unlock smartphones using fingerprints
   d) To provide navigation directions

4. In which area is Augmented Reality (AR) used to enhance learning?
   a) Education
   b) Healthcare
   c) Shopping
   d) Social Media

5. Which of the following is a typical application of Face Recognition technology?
   a) Creating virtual worlds
   b) Unlocking smartphones
   c) Adding digital elements to videos
   d) Showing directions on a map

Exercise 2 – Check if the sentence is true or false.

1. Virtual Reality (VR) overlays digital elements onto the real world. …………..
2. Computer Vision helps AI recognise objects in images and videos. …………..
3. Augmented Reality (AR) creates a completely new, immersive digital environment. …………..
4. Face Recognition technology is used to analyse medical images in healthcare. …………..
5. AI and VR serve the same purpose in creating digital experiences. …………

Exercise 3 – Fill the blank space with the correct word.

1. ………………… Reality (VR) creates a fully immersive digital environment.
2. ……………. is used to recognise and identify individuals based on their facial features.
3. In ………………. Reality (AR), digital elements are added to the real world.
4. ………………..Vision enables AI to interpret images and videos like a human would.
5. AR is commonly used in …………….. to make learning more interactive.

Exercise 5- Arrange the sentence in the correct sequence.

1. world / AR / elements / to / the / adds / digital / real.
2. used / to / images / Computer / Vision / analyze / is.
3. creates / VR / a / immersive / environment / digital.
4. for / is / healthcare / recognition / Face / used / technology.
5. intelligent / AI / tasks / helps / machines / perform.

Exercise 6- Carefully examine the group and circle the item that doesn't belong with the others.

1. Virtual Reality, Augmented Reality, Face Recognition, Digital Painting
2. Smartphone, VR Headset, Computer Vision, Controller
3. Navigation, Social Media Filters, Virtual Classroom, AI Programming
4. X-rays, MRIs, VR Games, CT Scans
5. Image Search, Face Recognition, AI Gaming, Self-Driving Cars

Exercise 7- Answer the following questions in your own words.

1. What is the main difference between AR and VR?
2. How does Computer Vision work in AI?
3. Name one way AR is used in education.
4. What is the purpose of Face Recognition technology?
5. How does VR differ from traditional video games?

Exercise 8- Look at the pictures below. Each photo shows a different technology: Augmented Reality (AR) or Virtual Reality (VR). Carefully observe the image and decide if it represents AR or VR. Write "AR" or "VR" in the box next to each picture.

....

....

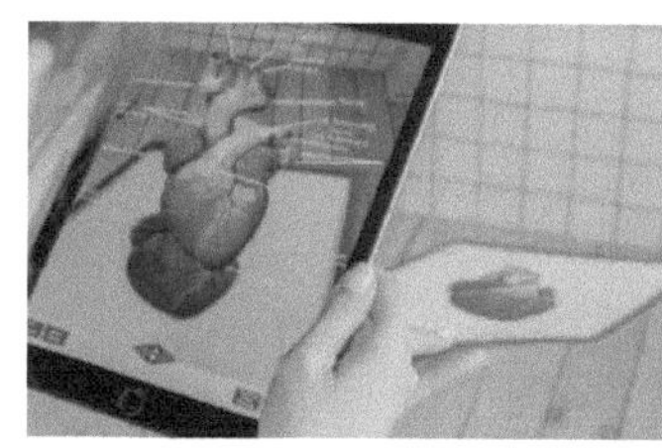

....

....

....

....

5.11 Project Work

Link: https://www.youtube.com/playlist?list=PLzlh_31VWEFoX2NdIPrJ-cZ3GMnsP6GOz

QR Code:

Create your own AR or VR experience.

To design a simple Augmented Reality (AR) or Virtual Reality (VR) experience using available tools or by creating a concept on paper.

5.12 Group Discussion

Link: https://www.youtube.com/playlist?list=PLzlh_31VWEFpkkG-qmcOSmkRG8-CnsaJr

QR Code:

The Impact of AR, VR, and AI on Our Future

The objective is to encourage students to think critically and collaboratively about the impact of AR, VR, and AI on the future. It helps students deepen their understanding, improve communication skills, explore ethical considerations, and foster teamwork as they discuss how these technologies can shape education, entertainment, daily life, etc.

5.13 Case Study

Link:https://www.youtube.com/playlist?list=PLzlh_31VWEFpSIUeGQZY3P14EklHmeFSF

QR Code:

The Future Classroom: AR or VR?

Scenario:

A school is considering using new technologies to make learning more exciting. The principal decides whether to invest in Augmented Reality (AR) or Virtual Reality (VR) for classroom activities. AR would allow students to see digital models on their desks using tablets, like a 3D volcano or historical landmarks. VR would take students on virtual field trips to faraway places, such as ancient Rome or the bottom of the ocean, using VR headsets.

Challenge:

The school has a limited budget and can only choose one technology now. The principal asks the students to help make the decision by discussing the pros and cons of AR and VR for learning.

5.14 Fun Activity

Activity: AI-Powered art gallery

Objective:

To introduce students to the creative possibilities of AI by generating artwork using AI tools or their imagination and then showcasing their creations in a classroom gallery.

Activity: Create and curate an AI art gallery

Preparation:

Provide students access to simple AI art generation tools (if available) or traditional art supplies like paper, markers, and coloured pencils.

Explain how AI can create art by analysing patterns, generating designs, or enhancing creativity.

Instructions:

AI-Generated Art (if tools are available): Students use an AI art tool to generate digital artwork. They can experiment with different styles, colours, and patterns to create something unique.

AI-Inspired Traditional Art (if AI tools aren't available): Students create artwork inspired by what they imagine an AI might produce. They can think about how AI sees the world and use abstract patterns, futuristic designs, or unusual colour combinations.

Gallery setup:

Once the artwork is complete, students help set up a classroom gallery. Each student displays their piece along with a short description of how AI inspired their work or how they used AI tools.

The class can view and discuss the artwork through the gallery.

Gallery tour and discussion:

As students tour the gallery, they take notes on their favourite pieces and think about how AI might influence art in the future.

After the tour, have a group discussion about the experience. Questions could include: "How did AI change how you created art?" or "What surprised you about the artwork?"

Reflection:

Students reflect on the role of AI in creativity and how it can be a tool for artists to explore new ideas and push the boundaries of traditional art forms.

Chapter-5

TEST PAPER
Augmented & Virtual Reality

Time Duration: 30 Minutes
Maximum Marks: 20

General Instructions:
1. This paper consists of twelve questions and is divided into two sections: A and B.
2. All questions are compulsory.
3. Section A comprises MCQs, Fill in the blanks, True or False, and One word of one mark each.
4. Section B comprises answer the following questions with three marks each.

SECTION-A

I - Choose the correct answer from the given options. **(1 X 2 = 2 marks)**

1. What does Virtual Reality (VR) primarily require to create an immersive experience?
   a) Smartphone
   b) VR Headset
   c) Computer
   d) Smartwatch

2. Which technology overlays digital information in the real world?
   a) Artificial Intelligence (AI)
   b) Virtual Reality (VR)
   c) Augmented Reality (AR)
   d) Computer Vision

II - Fill the blank space with the correct word. **(1 X 2 = 2 marks)**
1. Virtual Reality (VR) requires a ________ to immerse users in a digital environment.
2. ________ Reality (AR) adds digital elements to the real world.

III - Check if the sentence is true or false. **(1 X 2 = 2 marks)**
1. Virtual Reality (VR) can be used to simulate real-life experiences.
2. Augmented Reality (AR) completely replaces your natural surroundings.

IV - Write the answer in one word. **(1 X 2 = 2 marks)**
1. What technology overlays digital content in the real world?
2. What does VR stand for?

SECTION-B

V - Answer the following questions in your own words. **(3 X 4 = 12 marks)**
1. What is the difference between Augmented Reality (AR) and Virtual Reality (VR)?
2. How does Computer Vision help AI systems?
3. In what ways is AI used in daily life?
4. Why is Face Recognition technology i

Exercise 1- 1. b) 2. b) 3. b) 4. a) 5. b)
Exercise 2- 1. false 2. true 3. false 4. false 5. false
Exercise 3- 1. virtual 2. Face recognition 3. augmented 4. computer 5. education
Exercise 4-
1. AR adds digital elements to the real world.
2. Computer Vision is used to analyze images.

3. VR creates a fully immersive digital environment.
4. Face recognition technology is used for healthcare.
5. AI helps machines perform intelligent tasks.

Exercise 5- 1. Digital painting 2. Computer vision 3. AI programming 4. VI games 5. AI gaming

Online Resources

Online Exam Paper Link:
Link: https://forms.gle/MjWGNYNTYYURt5HV7
QR Code:

Chapter 5 Videos Link:
Link: https://www.youtube.com/playlist?list=PLzlh_31VWEFpaYOwcIKSJE8DPfW4-mRXi
QR Code:

More Sample Test Paper

Chapter 5 Test Paper – 1 Link:
Link: https://forms.gle/nwP3hisExPe9Eq23A
QR Code:

Chapter 5 Test Paper – 2 Link:
Link: https://forms.gle/HnzwghUwFz61j6dPA
QR Code:

Chapter 5 Test Paper – 3 Link:
Link: https://forms.gle/pBPSwA3KdGkfkVMq9
QR Code:

Chapter 5 Test Paper – 4 Link:
Link: https://forms.gle/dP8xEgFhzvG7Nyv57
QR Code:

ANNUAL TEST PAPER

Time Duration: 150 Minutes
Maximum Marks: 80

General Instructions:
1. This question paper consists of forty-four questions and is divided into four sections: A, B, C and D.
2. All questions are compulsory.
3. Section A comprises two passages carrying five marks each.
4. Section B comprises MCQs, fill-in-the-blanks, true or false, and one word of one mark each. The following terms are defined the following terms, carrying two marks each.
5. Section C comprises concise questions, which carry two marks each, and short answer-type questions, which have three marks each.
6. Section D comprises three questions. These are long questions that carry five marks each.

SECTION-A

I - Read the following passage and answer the questions that follow:
Artificial Intelligence (AI) is transforming education in remarkable ways. From personalised learning experiences to intelligent tutoring systems, AI is helping students learn more effectively. For instance, AI can analyse students' learning styles and adapt lessons to fit their needs, making education more tailored and accessible. In addition, AI-powered tools can assist teachers by automating administrative tasks, such as grading and attendance tracking, allowing them to focus more on teaching. However, the use of AI in education also raises questions about data privacy and the role of teachers in an increasingly automated classroom environment.

Questions:
1. How is AI helping students learn more effectively? **(2 Marks)**
2. What are some tasks that AI can automate for teachers? **(1 Mark)**
3. What is one concern about the use of AI in education? **(2 Marks)**

II - Read the following passage and answer the questions that follow:
Virtual Reality (VR) is revolutionising the entertainment industry by providing immersive experiences that transport users into new worlds. With a VR headset, users can find themselves in the middle of a thrilling adventure, whether exploring ancient ruins, fighting in a medieval battle, or navigating through a futuristic city. VR has expanded beyond gaming into other forms of entertainment, such as virtual concerts and interactive movies, where audiences can participate in the story. However, as VR technology becomes more advanced, it also raises concerns about the potential for addiction and the impact of prolonged use on mental health.

Questions:
1. How is VR changing the way people experience entertainment? **(2 Marks)**
2. Name two types of experiences VR offers beyond gaming. **(1 Mark)**
3. What is one concern related to the use of VR in entertainment? **(2 Marks)**

SECTION-B

III - Choose the correct answer from the given options. **(1 X 5 = 5 marks)**

1. What does AI stand for?
a) Automatic Intelligence
b) Augmented Intelligence
c) Artificial Intelligence
d) Advanced Intelligence

2. Which of the following is an example of AI in entertainment?
a) Face Recognition
b) Virtual Reality Gaming
c) Smart Thermostat
d) Voice Assistant

3. What is one feature of Human Intelligence?
a) Can recognize objects

b) Can create new ideas
c) Can store information
d) All of the above

4. AR stands for:
a) Augmented Reality
b) Artificial Reality
c) Advanced Reality
d) Automated Reality

5. Which of the following is a challenge in AI ethics?
a) Fairness
b) Privacy
c) Bias
d) All of the above

IV - Fill the blank space with the correct word. **(1 X 5 = 5 marks)**

1. ________ is a branch of AI that enables machines to recognise and interpret images.
2. Augmented Reality (AR) overlays digital elements onto the ________ world.
3. ________ is the technology used in devices like Siri and Alexa.
4. Virtual Reality (VR) typically requires a ________ to create an immersive experience.
5. ________ in AI is essential to ensure that the technology is used fairly and safely.

V - Check if the sentence is true or false. **(1 X 5 = 5 marks)**

1. AI can replace all human jobs in the future.
2. Virtual Reality creates a fully immersive digital environment.
3. Intelligence is only about solving mathematical problems.
4. AI in daily life includes applications like virtual assistants and smart home devices.
5. Computer Vision is not related to AI.

VI - Write the answer in one word. **(1 X 5 = 5 marks)**

1. What is the technology that creates fully immersive digital environments?
2. What do we call the ability of machines to perform tasks that usually require human intelligence?
3. What branch of AI allows machines to "see" and understand visual information?
4. Which technology adds digital information to the real world?
5. What is a typical example of AI used daily to answer questions?

VII – Define the following terms. **(2 X 5 = 10 marks)**

1. Artificial Intelligence (AI)
2. Augmented Reality (AR)
3. Virtual Reality (VR)
4. Computer Vision
5. Face Recognition

SECTION-C

VIII – Very short answer type questions. **(2 X 5 = 10 marks)**

1. What does Face Recognition technology do?
2. Which technology enhances the real world with digital elements?
3. What is the main ethical concern of AI?
4. Name one example of how VR is used in entertainment.
5. What branch of AI involves machines understanding visual information?

IX - Short answer type question. **(3 X 5 = 15 marks)**

1. Explain the difference between AI and VR.
2. How is AI used in healthcare?
3. Why is ethics important in AI development?
4. What are some examples of AI in everyday life?
5. How does AR enhance the shopping experience?

SECTION-D

X - Long answer type question. **(5 X 3 = 15 marks)**

1. Describe how Virtual Reality (VR) is used in education and training.
2. What role does Computer Vision play in developing self-driving cars?
3. Explain the potential impacts of AI on jobs and privacy.

More Online Annual Test Papers

Annual Test Paper – 1 Link:
Link: https://forms.gle/kAj7tbohTgguQjEf9
QR Code:

Annual Test Paper – 2 Link:
Link: https://forms.gle/Yn9orMexya5VQkvx5
QR Code:

Annual Test Paper – 3 Link:
Link: https://forms.gle/FvMYit2o6uPtD5ca8
QR Code:

Annual Test Paper – 4 Link:
Link: https://forms.gle/qkfgfQBwZsVZ4Lmg7
QR Code:

Tips for Solving Exam Papers

1. **READ THE ENTIRE PAPER**
   Quickly scan the paper to understand the questions and plan your time.

2. **START WITH EASY QUESTIONS**
   Answer the questions you find easiest first to build confidence.

3. **MANAGE YOUR TIME**
   Allocate time to each section and stick to it.

4. **UNDERSTAND THE QUESTION**
   Carefully read each question to ensure you know what's being asked before you answer.

5. **SHOW WORKINGS IN MATH**
   Always show your calculations to earn partial credit if needed.

6. **WRITE NEATLY**
   Present your answers clearly to make them easy to read.

7. **USE DIAGRAMS**
   Include diagrams where relevant, especially in Science.

8. **REVIEW YOUR ANSWERS**
   If time allows, review your answers to check for mistakes.

9. **ATTEMPT ALL QUESTIONS**
   Try to answer every question, even if you're unsure.

10. **STAY CALM**
    Stay relaxed and focused to think more clearly.

Chapter 6: Viva Voce

6.1 Questions and Answers

Question 1. What is Intelligence?
Answer. Intelligence is the ability to think, learn, and solve problems.

Question 2. Can AI replace humans?
Answer. AI can help humans by doing some tasks, but it cannot fully replace humans because it doesn't have feelings or creativity.

Question 3. How is AR used in learning?
Answer. AR can show 3D models of planets or animals that students can explore using their tablets.

Question 4. How does AI help doctors?
Answer. AI helps doctors by looking at X-rays or scans to find signs of diseases like cancer faster and more accurately.

Question 5. How is AI used in virtual assistants?
Answer. AI helps virtual assistants understand and respond to your questions, like asking Siri to set a reminder.

Question 6. What is a challenge in AI development?
Answer. A challenge is ensuring AI is unbiased and makes fair decisions for everyone.

Question 7. How does AI help in farming?
Answer. AI helps farmers by checking the health of crops and suggesting the best time to water or harvest them.

Question 8. What is a myth about AI?
Answer. It is a myth that AI will take over the world; AI is designed to help, not harm, humans.

Question 9. What is one way AI is used in your daily life?
Answer. AI helps by giving directions in Google Maps or suggesting songs on music apps.

Question 10. How does AI help in weather forecasting?
Answer. AI helps by analyzing weather data to predict things like rain or storms accurately.

Question 11. What is the role of AI in self-driving cars?
Answer. AI helps self-driving cars "see" and decide when to stop, go, or turn.

Question 12. How does AI help in language translation?
Answer. AI instantly helps apps like Google Translate convert text or speech from one language to another.

Question 13. What is a fun way AI is used in games?
Answer. AI controls characters in games, making them more innovative and more challenging to play against.

Question 14. What is the difference between Human Intelligence and Artificial Intelligence?
Answer. Human intelligence includes emotions and creativity, while AI can only follow instructions and learn from data.

Question 15. What is AI bias?
Answer. AI bias happens when an AI system makes unfair decisions favouring one group over another.

Question 16. How does AI help in Face Recognition?
Answer. AI scans your face and compares it to stored data to identify or verify your identity.

Question 17. How does AI help with online shopping?

Answer. AI recommends products you might like based on your previous searches or purchases.

Question 18. Why should we learn about AI?
Answer. We should learn about AI because it's becoming a big part of our lives, and understanding it helps us use it responsibly.

Question 19. What is a virtual reality experience?
Answer. A virtual reality experience is when you wear a VR headset and enter a completely different digital world, like exploring space.

Question 20. Can AI help with climate change?
Answer. Yes. AI can help by analysing data to predict weather patterns and suggest ways to reduce energy use and pollution.

6.2 Online Exam Paper

Link: https://forms.gle/4t66NUPVWVWhTZSg8
QR Code:

6.3 Online Video

Link: https://www.youtube.com/playlist?list=PLzlh_31VWEFrYeRqvPHjHxkclmyuWPu_n
QR Code:

Hello Riya, tell me What is AI used for in daily life?
Hello mam, AI helps with tasks like giving directions, making recommendations, and assisting with language translation.
How is AI used in gaming?
AI controls non-player characters, making games more challenging and interactive.
What is the role of AI in healthcare?
AI assists doctors by analyzing medical images and identifying diseases early.
How does AI help with security?
AI is used in facial recognition systems to identify people and enhance security.

So Aryan, tell me How does AI assist in agriculture?
AI helps farmers monitor crop health and suggests the best time for planting and harvesting.
How is AR used in education?
AR allows students to explore 3D models of objects, enhancing their learning experience.
What is the role of AI in self-driving cars?
AI helps cars navigate by recognizing surroundings and making decisions like stopping or turning.
What is a challenge AI faces?
One challenge is ensuring AI remains unbiased and fair to all users.

Additional Resources

CBSE Class 6 Artificial Intelligence Textbook Videos Playlist Link:
Link: https://www.youtube.com/playlist?list=PLzlh_31VWEFoDXegRF_6Y0y6R9jX1bzRr
QR Code:

Chapter 1 Video Playlist Link:
Link: https://www.youtube.com/playlist?list=PLzlh_31VWEFo0YjhqJwoN8tF9YcbsPI8X
QR Code:

Chapter 2 Video Playlist Link:
Link: https://www.youtube.com/playlist?list=PLzlh_31VWEFr_wPR2USYLq35na3Sf20Tk
QR Code:

Chapter 3 Video Playlist Link:
Link: https://www.youtube.com/playlist?list=PLzlh_31VWEFpe_kZBmjnQxMy7kO_G09yM
QR Code:

Chapter 4 Video Playlist Link:
Link: https://www.youtube.com/playlist?list=PLzlh_31VWEFpLoD0oi4NVOLnGHvCjf2Vz
QR Code:

Chapter 5 Video Playlist Link:
Link: https://www.youtube.com/playlist?list=PLzlh_31VWEFpaYOwcIKSJE8DPfW4-mRXi
QR Code:

Chapter 6 Video Playlist Link:
Link: https://www.youtube.com/playlist?list=PLzlh_31VWEFrYeRqvPHjHxkclmyuWPu_n
QR Code:

Project Videos Playlist Link:
Link: https://www.youtube.com/playlist?list=PLzlh_31VWEFoK-hIkEKTRDGc4VHy7KuNZ
QR Code:

Group Discussion Videos Playlist Link:
Link: https://www.youtube.com/playlist?list=PLzlh_31VWEFrFFYPmXPoqIydJwOB-TyHe
QR Code:

Case Study Videos Playlist Link:
Link: https://www.youtube.com/playlist?list=PLzlh_31VWEFp38OfCddIZsP-DmwWuAfoF
QR Code:

MCQs Playlist Link:
Link: https://www.youtube.com/playlist?list=PLzlh_31VWEFp4Z4NyJG3uRwbZcIWi5yOU
QR Code:

Fill in the blanks Playlist Link:
Link: https://www.youtube.com/playlist?list=PLzlh_31VWEFrm1U5pvYUjbdLLY0Z62C0Y
QR Code:

True or False Playlist Link:
Link: https://www.youtube.com/playlist?list=PLzlh_31VWEFpGU6K9HBHjtfg-kBrB6mQx
QR Code: